# PARENTING TEENS IN TODAY'S CHALLENGING WORLD 2-IN-1 BUNDLE

PROVEN METHODS FOR IMPROVING TEENAGERS BEHAVIOUR WITH POSITIVE PARENTING AND FAMILY COMMUNICATION

BUKKY EKINE-OGUNLANA

TCECPUBLISHING.COM

© **Copyright Bukky Ekine-Ogunlana 2021 – All rights reserved.**

The content contained within this book may not be reproduced, duplicated or transmitted without direct written permission from the author or the publisher.

Under no circumstance will any blame or legal responsibility be held against the publisher, or author, for any damages, reparation, or monetary loss due to the information contained within this book. Either directly or indirectly. You are responsible for your own choices, actions and results.

Legal Notice:

This book is copyright protected. This book is only for personal use. You cannot amend, distribute, sell, use, quote or paraphrase any part, or the content within this book, without the author or publisher's consent.

Disclaimer Notice:

Please note the information contained within this document is for educational and entertainment purpose only. All effort has been executed to present accurate, up to date, and reliable, complete information. No warranties of any kind are declared or implied. Readers acknowledge that the author is not engaging in the rendering of legal, financial, medical or professional advice. The content within this book has been derived from various sources. Please consult a licensed professional before attempting any techniques outlined in this book

By reading this document, the reader agrees that under no circumstances is the author responsible for any losses, direct or indirect, which are incurred as a result of the use of the information contained within this document, including, but not limited to, — errors, omissions, or inaccuracies.

## CONTENTS

### PARENTING TEEN GIRLS IN TODAY'S CHALLENGING WORLD

| | |
|---|---|
| Editor's Preface | 9 |
| Introduction | 13 |
| 1. Raising Teenage Daughters | 17 |
| 2. Effective Ways to Help Your Teens Cope | 24 |
| 3. Parenting Teenage Girls | 34 |
| 4. Breaking Through the Perpetual Glass Ceiling | 53 |
| 5. Breaking Stereotypes | 67 |
| 6. A Personal Story | 73 |
| 7. Teens in the World | 84 |
| 8. "Decoding" Your Teens and Helping Them Thrive | 98 |
| 9. Raising Daughters | 109 |
| Conclusion | 117 |
| Other Books You'll Love! | 121 |
| References | 131 |

### PARENTING TEEN BOYS IN TODAY'S CHALLENGING WORLD

| | |
|---|---|
| Introduction | 137 |
| 1. Techniques to Understand Your Teenage Son | 145 |
| 2. Fostering Creativity | 157 |

3. Handling Anger as a Parent 170
4. Methods to Discipline Teen Boys 177
5. Raising Teens 183
6. A Parent's Survival Guide to Teenage Boys 201
   Conclusion 235
   Other Books You'll Love! 241
   References 251

*Other Books You'll Love!* 255
*References* 263

*This book is dedicated to our three amazing children and all the beautiful children worldwide who have passed through the T.C.E.C 6-16 years programme over the years. Thank you for the opportunity to serve you and invest in your colourful and bright future.*

# PARENTING TEEN GIRLS IN TODAY'S CHALLENGING WORLD

## PROVEN METHODS FOR IMPROVING TEENAGERS BEHAVIOUR WITH WHOLE BRAIN TRAINING

EDITOR'S PREFACE

Whether you are a first-time parent to a daughter, or you've been here before, parenting girls takes patience, compassion, and love, just as it would for your son. However, girls have a different experience than boys and have to face a slew of barriers and hurdles that will come as they age. Devising a parenting technique to raise confident and strong-willed daughters can be difficult because parents, especially new parents, do not know where to begin. But do not fret! This Is precisely the reason that has driven the motivations to write this book. It is dedicated to parents everywhere who mean well and want the best for their children but feel like they are completely in, over their heads. A good thing to remember is that many parents share this feeling, but they can overcome this through perseverance and patience.

One thing to remember and always keep at the back of your mind is that parenting eventually becomes mostly instinctual. As much as you want to adhere to the tips outlined in this book, the best course of action is to absorb the knowledge presented in this book and bring it into your real life as you parent your children, regardless of what age they are. And as they continue to age and mature, it is essential to learn how to adapt and change with them.

The ideas presented in this book are general rules you can choose to apply to your life when parenting your children. From toddlers to teens, the tips presented in this book serve as assurances for parents unsure of what method to employ in their own lives. Ultimately, these methods are rooted in compassion and empathy. But the crucial thing to know is that every child is uniquely different. As I'm sure you have noticed within your child, every girl and every boy has varying perceptions of life and meets life's challenges differently. Discipline comes in many forms, and educating your children is not as universal as it might seem. Every child will experience their trials and tribulations that will shape them into a unique person.

As a result, parents have to understand this, and parenting has to reflect this accordingly.

You may find that some of the tips in this book do not apply to your child. More often than not, parenting takes trial and error. Parents sometimes forget this important detail and feel frustrated and demotivated when pushing their children down the right path. Instilling discipline, compassion, empathy, and kindness within children does not simply happen overnight. Parenting is a lifelong journey that never truly ends. So, the biggest tip that I can impart to any reader is to treat your children with respect and love that is never compromised. This is the foundational basis for good parenting.

This book is a must-read for prospective parents who are afraid of the unknown. It will set you up for a bright future ahead that prioritizes your children and their well-being. Parenting is a bumpy road, and you will experience extreme highs and the lowest of lows. This is all part of the journey that every parent encounters. This book will help you reflect on your choices in an intentional and meaningful way.

For parents who are deep in parenting trials, the ideas presented here will help you regain confidence in your abilities. It will help you turn around your situation for the better, especially if you are dealing with children who are acting out or going through a difficult time themselves.

Ultimately, this book serves to help parents provide the best possible environment for their children.

INTRODUCTION

While it is difficult to say if one gender is inherently more problematic to raise than the other, being a girl and more specifically, a teenage girl can be a tough and challenging time as the female body experiences extreme changes that can undoubtedly scare and even traumatize young girls. Many biological differences can affect both boys and girls, and for girls, hormonal changes can significantly impact a female's mental health and wellbeing. Additionally, societal expectations on the role of females limit them as they age. Females are subjected to glass ceilings and several biases that males will never understand.

For parents raising teenage girls, this can be a breeze for many as girls tend to be more resourceful and independent at this age than their male counterparts. However, that isn't to say that all girls are this way, and it certainly depends on the environment they are raised in and the childhood influences that play a massive part in shaping teens and their later years. Parents are faced with the typical teenage woes and have to deal with the set of problems that come with being a teenage boy or a teenage girl. In general, for adolescent girls, the social norm that has been established allows them to ask for help or receive help and affection. Facing emotional issues tends to be a more common problem seen in teenage boys.

So, when it comes to raising boys and girls, techniques catered to specific genders simply do not exist because the issues that each gender deals with can be so diverse and unique to each individual. Rather than seeing teen girls and boys in groups and adhering to stereotypes that make sweeping generalizations about how they may act, the more effective way is to see your child as an individual and treat them as such. This way, you can better understand the issues they may be facing and cater to their needs.

Seasoned parents would argue that teenagerhood is the most challenging time for parenting. Many parents might say that this period for your teenagers is a time of high emotions and added pressure as your teenager experience leaving their childhood and are on the cusp of adulthood. Your teens are in the process of making big decisions that will affect their futures, particularly with their educations and careers, which is an incredibly stressful time for most. Teens could be experiencing more complex relationships and the emotions associated with that. Additionally, as your children age, they become more accustomed to the fact that the world is more flawed than what they might have been used to during their protected childhood years that featured a far more idealistic and optimistic view. As your children age, they are met with the responsibilities they will have to take on as adults. With all of these in mind, the immense stress that can weigh on a teen's mental health during this time can be enormous. With this age transition being so formative and crucial for your teens, the same stress and pressure reflect on parents, which is why teenagehood is challenging for both parents and children alike.

However, that is not to say that techniques don't exist for raising respectable and good-hearted teens. It comes down to parents instilling these good values into their teens to carry these life lessons well into adulthood and practice them. As much as gender stereotyping should be discouraged, there are a few inherent differences between boys and girls that should be differentiated and discussed when raising girls and boys. However, keep in mind that all of the tips introduced in these books are interchangeable between genders and can be applied to any teen. They have no prerequisites or preconditions that need to be followed before being applied. These tips are universally applicable and really serve to nurture your teen's interests and needs, regardless of their gender.

These books are here to provide a framework for raising your teens. They are great resources to understand what your child may be going through during this especially volatile time. Refer to this books companion piece if you are raising a son and seek to understand the challenges they may face.

After reading this guide, please feel free to leave a review based on your findings and how useful the guide was to you. I would be incredibly thankful if you could take 60 seconds to write a brief review Amazon or the platform of purchase, even if it's just a few sentences!

## RAISING TEENAGE DAUGHTERS

*R*aising teenage daughters does not necessarily have to be a tricky thing. What becomes problematic is establishing the balance between the parent and child dynamic because of the inherent need to be an authoritative figure while maintaining a close connection with your daughter. Striking this balance is essential and one of the biggest challenges that parents face when raising their teenage daughters because of the extreme changes they are going through. While parents have to discover the best way to parent their kids, they also have to evolve alongside them and accept that times are changing where their children seek to be more independent by their terms during this stage of their lives. While their bodies are changing, so are their minds. Parents have to deal with the fact that their children simply do not require them as much as they did when they were younger and more reliant on them for their survival. This is the time for them to start dipping their toes in the water and finding their way through the challenges of life. Your kids must learn things by themselves and avoid feeding them the answers to everything.

While your teenage daughter is growing, the emotional impact that puberty has on a girl should not be underestimated. You will see changes manifest in many different ways, or perhaps even a combination of all of the following. Girls tend to be significantly underestimated, and their emotions tend to be brushed off because of the stereotypes that encourage a mindset that females are too emotional. Not only is this a dangerous mindset, but it also wholly sweeps all of the issues your daughter may be going through under the rug. It is essential to be perceptive of the changes they may be going through because they may not be immediately comfortable sharing these private details with you. It is equally important to listen to them and validate their feelings and act on them if they need help. Some parents may struggle with trying to identify if their daughter may be going through a hard time. Here are some signs to look out for if you suspect your teenage daughter is experiencing difficulty.

## 1. Changing tides

Physical developments and changes that puberty brings can trigger body and self-esteem issues for your teenage daughter. It is not uncommon for self-consciousness to manifest during this period as teens experience acne discomfort and other changes to their appearance. This can trigger a lifetime of harmful or self-destructive behaviour if not taken seriously from the get-go.

## 2. Mood swings

While TV shows and movies depict an often exaggerated and cliched version of how teenage daughters face mood swings, there is some truth to the stereotype as teen girls tend to show more varying degrees of sadness and happiness levels throughout their daily lives as societal expectations allow girls to be more expressive of their emotions and feelings. At the same time, males do not experience this in the same way.

## 3. Independence

Puberty does not just entail biological changes. As teenagerhood is a time to express independence, this can manifest in many different ways. Some girls may choose to dress differently and express themselves through their fashion. Some may decide to try out other hobbies or activities. The possibilities here are endless.

## 4. Body image

Body image impacts teen girls especially more profoundly and girls tend to focus on their outward appearances because of how drastic the changes can be. Additionally, the constant presence and availability of social media and edited pictures circulating the internet and have become commonplace create unrealistic expectations of beauty for young girls to aspire towards.

## 5. Friendships

Friend groups, particularly among girls, can sometimes be especially volatile. There is some truth in the stereotype of girls flocking in cliques. Your daughter may be on the receiving end of the negative aspect and might be experiencing loneliness or even alienation from their social circles. Knowing how your child is doing socially is especially crucial during these formative years because it can significantly leave a lasting negative impact if left unattended.

## 6. Relationships

At this age, teenagers may be acting on romantic impulses and experiencing their first loves and consequently, their first heartbreaks. I have seen these many times in the schools. This can be an extremely vulnerable time that may result in them going through difficult emotions as they grapple with new relationships and the pressures associated with a relationship. Good counselling and guide have helped in school and could benefit at home as well.

## 7. Bullying

Bullying can manifest in many forms during a teen's life. It can profoundly impact your teen's personality and behaviour that can follow them well into adulthood if not dealt with appropriately early on.

## 8. Peer Pressure

During this time, teens want to feel like they belong and are part of a group and identify with the people around them. But peer pressure can introduce its stresses and put your teens into uncomfortable situations that they might not be sure how to get out of.

## 9. Substance Use

Drugs and alcohol make themselves more known during this period of your teen's life. Peer pressure can play a massive impact in this as your teen might find themselves back into a corner where they feel like they have to try these dangerous substances. Or they may rely on alcohol or drugs to relieve the stress they may be experiencing.

## 10. Mental health

Whatever the cause may be, your teen's mental health will be impacted in some way during their most formative years. It can manifest in several negative ways, from social anxiety to depression. There are plenty of things that can affect a teen's mental health; from friends and social interactions, break up, parental pressures, academic pressures…the list goes on.

# Your free gift!

AS A WAY OF SAYING THANK YOU
FOR
PURCHASING THIS BOOK, I AM
OFFERING YOU A FREE GIFT AT THE
END OF THE BOOK

## EFFECTIVE WAYS TO HELP YOUR TEENS COPE

Once you have identified where your teen daughter might be struggling, developing a plan of action to help them cope with their problems can be too daunting and stressful as you ultimately want the best for your child. But it is essential if you're going to impart healthy and appropriate coping mechanisms into your daughter from a young age.

### 1. Self-image

The issues that arise out of self-image issues can be diverse and extreme. It can manifest in the form of eating disorders and body dysmorphia. While boys can also go through the same thing, girls experience an added pressure on their outward appearance during their teenage years. To cope with this, monitor your teen closely, especially at the dinner table. Notice their eating habits and make sure that they are getting plenty of fruits and vegetables. Have an open communication line to discuss how Photoshop can significantly alter how females look and that a person's worth is not based on how they look. Instil in them that being healthy is ultimately the most important thing.

Teach your daughter the importance of self-worth by encouraging her to have positive role models in her life. Positive role models could be anyone, from parents to teachers to friends. These models exist in their lives and show them how to cope with situations like growing up and facing the changes they are experiencing. Growing up, you get to figure out who you are by what other people tell you that you are until you begin to discover for yourself who you are.

One effective method to help your daughter with the way she views herself is to be cautious with the words you use around her.

It is more difficult for us as humans to place a lens on ourselves. Instead, what often happens is that our attitudes project onto another person. In this case, as parents continue to project a negative outlook, our children reflect this same negative attitude. And even when we look at the mirror, we tend to confirm what we have heard other people say about us. An excellent way to understand this is in the scenario of when someone tells you, "You have particles of food on your mouth". The immediate response here is to go to a mirror and check your reflection. When you notice that the food particles are there, your response is usually to remove it because the mirror has identified the problem you did not see by yourself.

Teens tend to approach mirrors with the opinion of others already ingrained in their minds. As adults, we have grown and matured to develop our views of ourselves. Still, young girls take everything said about them to that mirror and scrutinize themselves down to the smallest details to see if it is true, especially when it comes to negative comments. Even if it is not valid, they will look and look until they start to see what may not even be there. So, what can you do to help?

Speak scriptures, encouraging and uplifting words to your daughter. I am not just talking about the usual "you look beautiful today" because focusing solely on their looks teaches them to value themselves based on their appearances. Instead, please focus on the good habits and values they exhibit, such as hard work, persistence, and diligence. Notice how caring and creative they are and be sure to point out these strengths.

The critical thing to remember is that your words are the seeds that they take to the mirror. As they take it to the mirror, they will reconsider your comments, and their understanding of who they are continues to develop positively. When they go outside of the home environment, they may not receive good seeds (words) from others, where the real test lies. However, having the foundation of hearing positive and uplifting words from home will help them differentiate between what they can accept as true and false. Teens will begin to see that not everything everyone says about them is correct. Most teen girls do not know this, and it will be helpful to let them know the truth.

## 2. Relationship

This can be an exceptionally complicated thing to relate to your children because young love we see in schools can be innocent yet also problematic in its way. Especially from an adult's perspective, trying to relate to your teenage daughter's experiences can be doubly challenging, but this is the time to educate your teenage daughter on sex. Sex Education should by no means be a taboo subject because you want to be able to impart on her the importance of keeping herself. While schools have health subjects, it is important to teach her biological processes and give her a basic understanding of how pregnancy can happen. Be open and honest and share with her without sugar-coating things and do not treat this subject as taboo because it will be a sign to her to bottle up her feelings and feel ashamed. The absolute last thing you want for your daughter is to be ashamed and have a lifelong regret for making her own independent decisions.

When it comes to the area of relationships at a teenager's level, where do we even begin? Many parents think that talking with girls at a young age is enough to ensure that they will grow and continue developing as they deem it correct. However, parents must be more sensitive and in-tune with their teens' feelings and emotions in this modern age. There are two ways to which this conversation might go: it could be either too awkward for all the parties involved or just another simple conversation between a family.

One of the best ways to approach a subject of this magnitude is by highlighting it in its natural setting. For example, this can include bringing up the topic of friendships with boys after seeing your teen in a social environment and with that as the jumping-off point. You can branch out into a more in-depth conversation. The aim here is to inform your child of certain boundaries while also understanding their relationships at a romantic capacity.

For many mothers and their daughters, this conversation ends up being difficult because it can lead to a lot of embarrassment from both parties. But the reality is that the conversation needs to be had. Making this a taboo subject only closes doors for open discussion and talks.

### 3. Bullying

This can be a challenging subject for your daughter to broach because of a myriad of reasons. They may feel ashamed or scared of the consequences. They may think that bullying is their fault and may not understand that they do not deserve to be bullied. Ensure that you have a strong foundation with your daughter to recognize if she is shutting down or being more closed-off. This can be an indication that she is being bullied. Broaching the subject with her can be difficult. She may not feel comfortable sharing the details but reassuring her that you will support her and try your best to help her out of this challenging situation can significantly ease the stress. Give her advice on how to face bullying and stand up for herself. If the issue is more severe, it may be time to step in and have a serious talk with her school. This is where parents come in and directly intervene with your child's time at school and have a serious discussion with the teacher. Sometimes having proof might even help the case. If this is an instance of cyberbullying, saving screenshots to show to the administration and authorities (if need be) can help further the issue from just a reprimand to more severe punishment to the perpetrator.

## 4. Education

Teenagerhood can be a doubly stressful time for your kids' education because they are inching closer and closer to college and university. This added pressure can significantly affect your child's performance, and more often than not, children can feel like their self-worth is tied to the grades they get. To tackle this, reassuring your child that you value hard work and effort more so than grades. Low grades are not an indicator of any person's self-worth and consider finding an outlet for your child to engage in to destress and relax after school.

While watching your child struggling is difficult, simply handing them the answers is even worse. Don't be overprotective over your daughters and let them make mistakes. A big part of developing a resilient sense of self-worth is the ability to bounce back from the obstacles that life presents. So, the next time your daughter is struggling to cram for an exam she had weeks to study for, don't merely bail her out and give her the easy way out. Allow her to learn from her mistakes and face the ramifications of her errors, which, as she will learn, does not mean that everything comes crashing down. Facing the consequences and overcoming challenges is part of becoming a resilient adult. Differentiate between being her support system and someone who simply cleans up her messes.

### 5. The power of "no."

It is also crucial to educate your daughter, above all else, the power of the word "no". Saying "no" can help your daughter out of situations and can even save her life. Your daughter has every right to say "no", especially when she is uncomfortable, and while all parents would agree with this, many do not enforce this enough with their daughters. Prioritize teaching them this in their development. Your teens may need to practice this a few times with their family members to get comfortable with the idea of asserting their feelings but doing so is an excellent way to get accustomed to politely but firmly refusing someone.

## 6. Substance Use

Educate your kids about the detrimental side effects of drugs and alcohol, in addition to the consequences they face from illegal consumption as they are underage. Some teens in a discussion in the class argued that the best way to combat this is to allow them to experience it in a controlled environment, like under their parent's supervision. (The first trial is the only trial needed to be addicted)

Teen girls are more vulnerable to developing alcohol and drug problems due to their greater susceptibility to peer pressure. Their surroundings and environmental stress is often the cause that leads teen girls to succumb to substance usage. Teen girls tend to turn to substances to cope with existing issues. Pay close attention to their moods to see if anything has changed or if they appear any different. Drastic mood changes can indicate that your teen is experimenting with drugs or alcohol. If you suspect so, take action immediately from a professional as their health and safety could be at risk.

PARENTING TEENAGE GIRLS

These techniques can be interchangeable with parenting teen boys as parenting, in general, requires being compassionate and empathetic to your child's struggles. These tips are a great place to start if you are unsure how to transition from raising a young girl to an adolescent. Ultimately, there is no "one size fits all" approach for raising a son or daughter, and it may take some trial and error to find the perfect fit of balancing discipline and being their friend. Here are some tips for dealing with the challenges that raising a teenager can bring:

## 1. Communication is key

A lot of grief can be saved if your children simply communicate what they may be going through. But this just is not the case because of the complexities of emotions your teens are faced with. They might feel scared or intimidated and fear punishment or shame if they were to share their true feelings, which means that it falls onto the parent to connect with their teens as much as possible and be an avid listener. Establish yourself as a trusted confidant and a safe space to share their deepest and darkest concerns.

Cindy and her daughter Lilly shared a close bond ever since Lilly was young. During Lilly's teen years, her mother's relationship suffered because she found herself developing new interests that differed from her mother's. This was difficult for Cindy because she had grown so used to Lilly's companionship as her daughter and friend. Communication lines that were once wide open diminished every day as Lilly grew increasingly secretive with her new friends in high school and the new things that interested her in life. She simply did not want to share with her mother what she and her friends were up to.

For Cindy, re-establishing communication was the challenge she had to face. Through trial and error, she did so by finding a new hobby for her and her daughter to pursue. Gardening became a hobby of choice. What first felt like manual labour to Lilly turned into a period she looked forward to every weekend to spend time with just her and her mother. Cindy was initially met with a lot of resistance as Lilly said she would rather spend time with her friends than with her mother. While the words were extremely hurtful, Cindy knew not to take it to heart. She knew that teens said things that they regretted and making mistakes was part of life. And she was validated when the next day Lilly came to apologize for her harsh words. Cindy had established trust and respect from Lilly's early days as a child, and here it was blossoming right before her eyes.

The fact is that Lilly had simply grown out of the hobbies she had loved to do with her mother. This was where Cindy realized that as a parent to a growing child, a teen no less, you might have to adapt and change as your child does to keep up with them. While Lilly loved doing the hobbies like cooking and baking as a child, she no longer liked them and found that this was the basis of her relationship with her mother, which is why she continuously pushed away from her as she aged and entered high school.

Once Cindy established a new neutral zone, it took some time for Lilly to recognize that her mother ultimately cared about her and was not someone who was going to judge her. By Cindy maintaining the boundaries between herself and Lilly and not being too pushy, she was able to get Lilly to open up after a few weeks of gardening together. She found out that Lilly struggled with insecurities and found difficulty coping with school and the new friends she was making. Being able to open up to her mother was crucial, and she realized how big of a hole it had left when she didn't have her mother to rely on and always pushed her away.

While parents may have strong and solid foundations established with their children that they anticipate will always be in place, this certainly isn't the case. The truth is that these foundations can be knocked down if you aren't paying attention. Details in behaviour and attitude can be a massive giveaway to how your child is doing if you pay attention and know what to look for. This means that you have to be wise to your child all the time. Sometimes communication lines can go out, so it is up to parents to figure out how to rewire the connection lines to get their kids to open up to them again. This takes a lot of patience and trust, but with a solid foundation, your kids will eventually come around.

## 2. Establish rules

Having realistic and logical boundaries that are concise and age-appropriate is crucial during this stage because teens want to challenge everything around them as they experience independence for the first time in their lives. Always expect that your rules will be broken, so be prepared with age-appropriate consequences that will teach your teens a lesson in a sustainable and effective way.

The punishments you dole out to your children will differ as they age. For example, if your child demonstrated lousy behaviour as a toddler, a common punishment that suited this was a time-out in the corner or perhaps taking away a privilege like watching TV. As a teen, time-outs definitely won't have the same effect. You might succeed in humiliating your teenager, but this will only develop even more resentment and foster frustration towards you. Instead, a parent to a teen might take a more "adult" approach to the time-out by perhaps cutting your teens curfew and making it earlier or banning them from using electronic devices. Taking away privileges as a punishment is an effective way to get through to your kids because it effectively forces them to listen to you when the things they enjoy are in jeopardy.

The tricky part is setting boundaries itself. Setting overcomplicated boundaries will only succeed in forcing your kid to ignore them and go about their way. For example, contradicting yourself and continuously changing the rules will eventually wear your child down so much that they choose to ignore the rules you have set. Avoid doing so by discussing boundaries with your children before setting them. Getting them involved in the process is an excellent way to gauge their expectations and how you can still respect their wishes and form a fair compromise for everyone involved. For example, curfews are a contentious subject for teens because while they want to stay out as late as possible, parents are expected to stay up waiting for their kids to return home. The expectation there is unfair towards parents and everyone else in the household. So in this case, coming to a compromise about a reasonable curfew is an excellent way to make sure that your teens both respect it and adhere to it.

## 3. Don't take bad attitudes and behaviour personally

As much as your teen's words can hurt and cut deep, try your best not to take it personally. This does not mean that they will not receive consequences for being disrespectful but be prepared to be argued with and have your buttons pushed continuously as your teens test the boundaries and fight against any form of authority or control.

## 4. Healthy risks

While children are attracted to pushing the boundaries and taking risks, this can be performed healthily. Through travelling, physical challenges and new social situations, there are plenty of ways to take healthy risks without endangering themselves or their health. Furthermore, parents have a better understanding of what their children might be up to when they engage in these activities, which significantly eases the mind. Encouraging these activities also broadens your child's horizons and diversifies their experiences and exposes them to many new and healthy coping ways.

## 5. Compromise

As much as you have a developed relationship with your teens and try your best to create a parenting style that fits them best, sometimes you might have to compromise with your teen's whims that may seem outlandish. Sometimes you may have to accept that this is another way for them to express themselves during this time. While you cannot control every single outcome, finding a happy medium and compromising with your teen is a way to try and maintain some semblance of calm and happiness.

## 6. Express love and affection

Unconditional love is precisely that. Your children will continuously make mistakes and push the boundaries, and you will as well as you try to help them navigate through their lives and face the challenges that will be presented. No one has the perfect answer or response to everything. What is crucial is that you take these mistakes and turn them into learning lessons for your kids to set an example of how to respond to situations of extreme emotions appropriately. Likewise, the backbone of everything you do when raising children is to practice unconditional love. This should not be leveraged or withheld because your child is exhibiting frustration or challenging behaviours.

### 7. Express how you feel

As your teens are older and more mature, they can relate to the emotions you may be feeling more so than they would have as a child. Being open and vulnerable to your children can significantly encourage them to do the same when trying to understand what they are going through. By sharing your struggles, your children can see that adults make mistakes and are susceptible to challenges. Being open with your kids encourages them to want to share more because you are setting a clear example of sharing their feelings and avoiding bottling them up. This can eventually implode and lead to unhealthy ways of coping and mental health issues like depression and anxiety.

### 8. Be compassionate

Your teen is experiencing struggles that to you may seem minute, but for them can be astronomical. Be compassionate to their struggles and try not to judge them too harshly as a young age tends to be a slew of bad decision making and reckless behaviour. Try and think of how you thought when you were that age look how far you have come in your thinking and understanding they too are yet to make that same journey. Instead, provide them with the support they need; whether it's a shoulder to cry on or someone to keep them company while they go through the consequences they face.

**9. You won't always be right**

Accept when you are wrong. Parents often struggle with this because they are so accustomed to telling their kids specifically what to do, and they may be met with resistance as they age and enter adolescence. Take time to evaluate the situation, and sometimes, you may be wrong too. It is far more effective and commendable to admit when you are wrong, as painful as it may be when you are in the face of an argument with your child, but it is the right thing to do.

**10. Trust their judgement**

As difficult as it may be relinquishing your hold on your kids, it is a natural consequence of your children growing up. When this happens, give them the freedom to act on their own choices and trust that they are making the most informed choice. Parents often want to step in and tell their kids exactly what to do, but should they make a mistake, it turns into a learning lesson for them to take with them for the next time and the rest of your life.

## 11. Choose your battles

It is true that raising teens bring a lot of butting heads and arguments. Sometimes you have to let it be. Picking a fight every single time is not only frustrating for both parent and child, but it can also encourage teens to want to rebel even more as your rules get stricter and increasingly tight. Pick your battles wisely and save yourself another day of arguments and fighting. Sometimes allowing your teens to decide things for themselves as long as they are not harming themselves or those around them is a way of compromising with the fact that they are growing up and making their own choices.

## 12. Focus on positivity

Positive encouragement is a tried-and-true method to get your kids to feel more confident in themselves. Especially when your child is going through a hard time, this can be a reminder that not all moments will be challenging and emotionally draining. Spending time with family and friends or pursuing their hobbies can give them a break from stressors and temporarily give teens a chance to focus on something else, rather than constantly obsessing over the issue at hand. If it's an appropriate time, try to encourage your teen to get away from the chaos and focus on something that they love to do to briefly take their minds off of things and help them clear their heads. While this is not a way to completely solve problems, it relieves stress, impacting overall mental health.

## 13. Recognize their rights

Parents often view their children as young and impressionable, which causes them to indulge their kids, even as they are in their teenage years. This stunts their development and fosters resentment as children do not feel seen or heard as individuals because they are continually being treated as children and not being given the freedoms they feel like they deserve. Recognize that your children are growing up and that they deserve freedoms in this process. They are no longer babies whose every move has to be tended to and watched. Allowing your kids to explore the world on their own enables them to grow and flourish in their way.

## 14. Respect goes both ways

While you expect your teens to respect you as an authority figure, respect their choices as well. Particularly during their teen years, your child may experiment and dabble in a new identity, whether that is through fashion or their interests. It can manifest in many ways. Frustration can build when parents choose not to validate this new identity. While it may be a phase, it can also potentially not be. Treat your kids with the same respect that you expect for yourself. Respect their choices and understand that you may not like everything they do, and they will not always turn to you for advice. Despite this, you should not hold a grudge or treat them any lesser than they are.

## 15. Professional help

Consider speaking to a professional if you find that you cannot grasp what your teen might be going through, whether it is because of reluctance on your teen's part to share or if the issue is more severe than you can help her manage. There is no shame in seeking professional help because it gives your teen a neutral party to speak to who provides a safe, judgement-free space for them to express themselves. This does not mean you are any less of a parent; it makes you a commendable one for recognizing your strengths and weaknesses and ultimately placing your child's health over your ego. Many parents struggle with the blow that their ego faces for they believe that speaking to a professional means that they are not a good parent. This is definitely not the case. Many teens recognize their parents' limitations and appreciate the degree of seriousness they treat their mental health.

Siblings are an essential subject that should be discussed when it comes to raising teenagers. Your child's siblings play a huge role in shaping and moulding them into the person they are, alongside your influence as a parent. For parents with multiple children, the dynamic in your household is one of the most important things. A dynamic that is not balanced will be met with a lot of chaos. This might look like one child getting more attention than the other or one child getting more leniency than their sibling. The list goes on and on. Without striking a balance between all the siblings, you risk breaking down the foundations that you worked so tirelessly to build among all your children.

Mina was a mother of two before becoming a mother to three children very unexpectedly. Her goddaughter Rosie entered into the family's lives without much warning, throwing the entire family dynamic out of balance because Mina's children Anna and Leah now had a new sibling. With more children meant less time divided between each of them. The beginning stages of the family was rough as they tried to make Rosie's unexpected appearance work. As happy and thrilled as they were about gaining a new daughter, Mina and her husband Jeremy were concerned about money becoming tighter now that they had another mouth to feed. While they never let it show and provided for all their children with as much joy and love as they could, their financial troubles were weighing them down. But Jeremy and Mina agreed never to tell their children and burden them with adult problems.

However, Anna, Leah, and Rosie were perceptive of their parents and could see that they were under a great deal of stress. But despite acknowledging this, Anna and Leah found it increasingly difficult to spend time with their parents as they once had. They were always working, and if they weren't, they were helping Rosie with something or another. On the other hand, Rosie was going through a rough patch as she had to very abruptly leave her old life behind and permanently join her godparents' family.

Families tend to go through a struggle in the beginning as they attempt to figure things out. In Mina's family's case, the battle was doubly difficult as they were dealing with a new addition to their family, financial troubles and trying to have all of the siblings bond together at the same time. Jealousy was bound to brew, and that is precisely what happened.

Rosie was experiencing difficulty herself as she attempted to join the family while dealing with her past trauma of leaving her home abruptly to join a new one that felt hostile from her new siblings. She made constant comments about being maltreated compared to the family's birth children and Shut down emotionally and refused to share her feelings.

The issues seemed to be compounding until everything finally came to a head one day that forced an entire family intervention. Mina and Jeremy were able to identify that the family dynamics had been compromised and were not getting any better. No one was benefiting from this family dynamic because no one felt supported or cared for. Everyone was more concerned with their issues and continued to retreat into their corners instead of bringing people closer. The problems were immense and unsolvable in one day.

The good news is that the issues were solved over the next few months. The family dynamic was altered to which everyone was now supportive of one another. No one felt neglected because everyone was able to voice their concerns honestly and without any filters. By doing so, Mina and Jeremy's household was a lot calmer for everyone involved. Eventually, when Mina and Jeremy were able to get back on track financially, they could spend some time finding resources for Rosie to help her cope with the trauma she experienced from being abruptly taken away from the comfort of her own home and into a new and unknown place. And while Rosie was in therapy, Jeremy and Mina worked out schedules to spend time individually with Anna and Leah. This time was rewarding because it gave them a chance to spend time with their parents one-on-one like they had never experienced before.

Furthermore, spending time with their parents meant open communication lines where they could voice their concerns. This was a space for Jeremy and Mina to patiently explain that compassion and empathy were essential traits to have, especially when someone new like Rosie enters their lives. While Anna, Leah and Rosie have grown closer and developed a sibling dynamic of their own, that isn't to say that it was an easy task by any means.

It took a collective effort from everyone's part to make the family work, which is the key takeaway from this story. A collectivized effort showed less than enthusiastic members that this was something they had to spend time working at because everyone else was doing so. Understandably, there were plenty of hiccups along the way, but as the famous African proverb goes: "It takes a village to raise a child". And the adage very much applies here to each of the children. Everyone was going through their issues that plagued the family dynamic as a whole. It took the whole family to sit down and re-evaluate their situation to make substantial changes that would benefit every family member.

For Mina, raising daughters in a family context meant identifying the most important values to the whole family. She wanted to be able to convey these values, mostly by example. It was imperative to model the values in daily life that she wanted her daughters to learn. Emulating the traits and strengths like kindness, gentleness, faithfulness, self-control, perseverance and tolerance were the qualities she wanted her daughters to develop as they grew, which is why it was so important to reflect these qualities in how she parented.

BREAKING THROUGH THE
PERPETUAL GLASS CEILING

*T*een girls face countless limitations within a patriarchal society that tells them what they can or cannot do. This is the reality of what females face in the real world, and these can eventually develop into full psychological roadblocks that your children will have to face in their adulthood. As their parent, it is your responsibility to forewarn your daughters of the realities and vulnerabilities that girls have to face outside of the household. These differences between genders are further fostered when your child enters the education system, mainly seen through the many education systems that segregate boys and girls during physical education classes. While education systems differ worldwide, the school system is often where these notions of gender and the applicable stereotypes are established within your child. By the time your child has entered their teen years, ideas of "running like a girl" or "acting like a boy" have firmly wormed their way into their mindset. It is an inevitable result of the education system.

The glass ceiling is an invisible barrier that prevents women from reaching the same potential as their male counterparts. Women often feel the impact of this early on, particularly in their teen years as they are establishing their education and career. Your daughter will immediately notice male domination the minute she enters into the real world. Rather than stifle her and scare her, be ready to fight these obstacles presented to her by being a constant support system and shoulder to cry on. Being someone, she can turn to for advice is also crucial for her when faced with difficult decisions that she has to make.

The road ahead will not be easy, especially if she enters predominantly male-dominated fields.

You may notice overlap of the following tips from the companion book entitled *Parenting Teen Boys in Today's Challenging World*. These tips are applicable regardless of your child's gender and should be seen as cardinal rules to successfully raising children.

These are especially appliable in breaking the glass ceiling for girls because it establishes stability and good role models for them to model after.

Here are some ways to set your daughter up to break her way through the glass ceiling. This will prepare her to face the challenges she will encounter head-on.

## 1. Build self-confidence from an early age

Develop a strong sense of self from an early age within the household. With the teen years being so divisive and stress filled, being sure of oneself can significantly reduce the impact these problems can bring. Rather than raising your child as a people pleaser, teach her to stand up for what she believes in and encourage her to use her voice. The realities of society will soon shut her down and often speak over her, so relying on her self-esteem and confidence will take her far as it will require her to use her voice unabashedly. Developing this early on can make this an inherent part of who she is once she enters teenagerhood.

## 2. Direct your praise to her achievements, rather than appearance

Females tend to have an obsession with their view because we are always surrounded by it in society. Rather than focusing on how she looks, focus on her achievements and how she is doing academically, morally and character-wise. This does not mean that you should never compliment your daughter on her appearance, but it does mean to be conscious of the unintentional focus people tend to have on women. Establish early on that your daughter is so much more than how she looks, and her self-worth is not tied to her appearance or how conventionally beautiful she is. Establish that beauty comes in many forms. Inner beauty is most crucial as it is gold. You should clothe yourselves instead with the beauty that comes from within, the unfading beauty of a gentle and quiet spirit, which is so precious to God (1 Peter 3:4)

## 3. Be affectionate

Demonstrating warmth and affection to all your children equally, regardless of gender, this allows them to feel a sense of security and comfort whenever they are in your presence. This ties in with giving them the courage to share what they may be going through as affection tells them that their parents will still love them regardless of their mistakes.

## 4. Avoid the "boys will be boys" mentality

This dangerous mentality is often used as an excuse to brush off certain behaviours or attitudes seen in boys. Teaching your daughters that men have to be held equally accountable for their actions allows them to see consequences for inappropriate behaviours. This also ties in with a girl's self-worth, as valuing yourself means protecting yourself from people who might want to take advantage of you. In this regard, teaching girls that there is never an excuse for inappropriate behaviour encourages them to speak out and put an end to people getting away with unacceptable behaviours.

## 5. Be present

While parents are expected to loosen the reins, it by no means entails completely abandoning parenting altogether. You represent a guide for your child to follow and model after, even into their adult lives. Being present in their lives means continuing the relationship and bond you share, even if you may feel like they simply do not need you anymore. Particularly when your daughter is attempting to break through the glass ceiling, having the unconditional and constant support of their parents reiterates that they are doing the right thing and will always have some form of stability even if their attempts at equality fail.

## 6. Be a guide

Your children look to you as their role model from the minute they are brought into this world. Especially for mothers, daughters look to you to see how you fight the everyday biases imposed onto you. Model for them how you would want them to act when faced in the same situation, regardless of how young they may be. Children are inclined to mimic their parents and recreate their behaviours because it is the best reference point. This way, you provide her with solutions to everyday problems that she will inevitably face as a teen daughter. Always be extremely conscious that your children are always watching you and by the time they are teens, they will use your behaviour as an argument should you stray away from the action or attitude you are trying to impart on them.

## 7. Claiming worth

Form an early age, teach your daughters to evaluate their beauty and competence by their maker's terms. Your daughters will try to avoid tying their self-worth to frivolous things and terms set by other people by encouraging this. Instead, they follow the laid down standard from their maker's perspective and create their standards to live by and determine what they deserve, despite the noise that will continuously bring them down and tell them they are lesser than.

## 8. Embrace a growth mindset

Because teens are so susceptible to mistakes, encouraging a "growth mindset" rather than a "fixed" one teaches your kids to learn from their mistakes and treat them as a learning lesson to develop themselves. This way, rather than focusing on the fact that they were wrong, focus on what exactly they did. Should they be faced with the same situation, they will better understand how to respond appropriately. Ultimately, we are all human and while finding our purpose in life is complicated but can be made easier by studying, reading and rereading scriptures spending 1-2 minutes allows the idea of God's presence settle around one, praying back God's truths, personalizing known truth, practising God's presence by recognizing that He is with you, meditating and obeying scriptures. We are creatures that learn and can expand, diversify and grow; mentally spiritually and socially.

## 9. Make room for failure

Failure can be extremely disappointing at this young age because teens tend to fixate on being an outlier as they want to fit in and be part of a group. Rather than glossing over the fact that they have failed something or avoiding a discussion about it, teach them to approach it head-on to face their fears and frights and get used to confronting these uncomfortable and less than ideal aspects of life. Getting used to failing sets them up for a life of unexpected failures, and having a healthy way of coping with them from an early age will help them much in the long run.

## 10. Focus on extending compassion

Encourage your children to treat themselves with kindness and acceptance. Self-loathing and hatred can manifest during these early ages of teenagerhood because your kids simply don't know how to cope with everyday life pressures, their academic performance and their changing bodies. These are huge stressors that weigh your teens down heavily. Rather than focusing on what they may be achieving all the time, focus on the language they use on themselves. Teach your teens to focus on their well-being by extending the kindness they would treat others with upon themselves. Understanding that every person is flawed and that we will never please every person we meet is something that we have to grapple with and get used to from a young age.

## 11. Avoid comparisons

Parents sometimes feel inclined to compare our kids to how our neighbour's kids might be doing. Everyone is at different aspects of their journeys, and we have to respect that our children will go through their unique journey. Rather than comparing them to others, compare your kids with where they were last year. Encourage them by pointing out how much they have developed in character and matured. Focus on spiritual, educational and self-development in a healthy and sustainable way.

## 12. Social media

Platforms like Instagram can have a negative impact on the way your teen views herself and her self-worth. It also places a significant emphasis on appearance. Social media and the concept of "likes" can seriously affect your child's development and foster jealousy and envy, leading to depression and anxiety. Encourage them to take breaks away from social media by nurturing their hobbies and interests.

## 13. Problem-solving

Encourage your daughters to solve her issues on her own rather than fixing things for her. Parents tend to take over because of their years of experience and knowledge, but girls don't develop the coping skills they need to handle situations independently. This is the time to ask your daughter to come up with her strategies or deal with a problem, and then let her decide what she wants to do. Even if you disagree with her choice and know its incorrect, give your daughter a sense of control over her own life and show her that she is responsible for her decisions.

## 14. Encourage her to take physical risks.

Girls are not dainty and should be allowed to get hurt and play in the mud as boys do. By letting girls take physical risks, she will develop stronger self-esteem because she can face challenges with confidence. Encourage your daughter to go beyond her comfort zone. This can look like putting her in a new sport or encouraging her to take small risks when riding her bicycle. Give her small challenges to conquer first so that she can grow more accustomed to pushing herself. Even non-athletic girls should develop some experience when it comes to physical activity while they are young. Forming a physical relationship with their body allows them to build confidence and get to know their limits even better.

## 15. Avoid drama

Catty behaviour or girl fighting has been long associated with girls and high school. If you have spotted it as a parent, it's a good idea to address it immediately to nip it in the bud. Catty behaviour is immature and childish. Gossip, rumour-spreading, exclusion and physical violence like hitting are behaviours that are not tolerated and should be stopped if it ever occurs. This does not mean that all girls have a mean streak in them and automatically want to gossip pull other girls' hair. However, this is a typical behaviour found in high school that should not be encouraged by any means. Suppose you find that your daughter is engaging in this mean-spirited behaviour. In that case, it's time to have a serious sit-down about bullying and practice more positive ways to change their relationships.

Adolescence is a time filled with self-doubt, and for many teen girls, this may be a time of struggle as they view themselves with a new light of insecurities. Early on, establishing with your kids that their self-worth is not directly tied with their outward appearance is an important lesson that needs to be learnt. For your daughters to feel confident in their convictions, employ these strategies that encourage self-growth and improvement and focus on efforts rather than immediate outcomes. Teaching your daughters to be assertive and having the ability to speak up for themselves in an appropriate way that will help re-establish a sense of confidence within themselves. A teen who can speak up for themselves is also less likely to be bullied or bullied for very long because their self-worth is perceived in a different and positive light. As it has been reiterated, the best way for your kids to understand and grasp this behaviour and attitude quickly is if parents themselves model this behaviour to have a first-hand view of how confidence and self-assuredness can significantly benefit them. Facing situations with courage helps your teen in the long run.

The most challenging aspect of encouraging positive thinking is to instil in your teens to think positively about themselves. A person's inner monologue plays a critical role in how they perceive themselves, and sometimes it seems easier to criticize and pick apart every little flaw that you may see in the mirror. Rather than doing this, encourage your teens to be kind to themselves and avoid being overly harsh on themselves. Try telling them, "You would never say these cruel and unkind words to anyone else, so why is it okay to say them to yourself?" developing a healthy and positive inner monologue can be difficult because our minds automatically want to gravitate towards the negative as we notice the flaws first. But with the support of parents and open discussion about what teens may think of themselves, this is a great way to teach your children to put a positive spin on things and be more optimistic about how they perceive themselves in their environment. For example, reframe thoughts like, "I'm not capable of doing this," into something more positive like, "I'm going to try my best and learn from my mistakes."

People often underestimate how much our thoughts can affect our ability, but by simply changing the way we think, we can have a more profound and positive impact on how we end up performing. Most of the time, a positive spin is met with reluctance. But try it for yourself and see how changing your mentality can have a direct correlation to how you end up performing.

Ultimately, it lies within the parent to teach their child to love themselves for who they are and not tie their worth to the number of followers they may have on Instagram or fit into that smaller jeans size. Building self-worth on a healthy foundation is the key to its sustainability. Emphasize the essential values like kindness, compassion, empathy and respect for others as the primary benchmarks for a person's self-worth.

## BREAKING STEREOTYPES

*J*ust like how there are many hobbies or interests that have been deemed "too girly" for men, the same can be said for women where their abilities are severely underestimated for specific activities and thus deemed unable to perform at the same standard of males. Not only is this false and an incredibly problematic generalization, but it also severely limits the capabilities of both males and females. These are great hobbies to encourage your teen girls to pursue that might seem "unconventional" but have significant mental and physical health benefits. Helping your teens build new skills redirects their focus from daily stressors like social media in a healthy and productive way.

## 1. Martial arts

Being able to verbally assert themselves or de-escalate a situation is a good starting point, but sometimes your teen may be in a vulnerable spot where they will have to use physical force. Learning self-defence as a young teen is particularly helpful and can potentially save your daughter's life. Aside from this, being successful in martial arts requires a high level of discipline and focus. It encourages individuals to use their physicality and improve them to grow stronger and keep your kids moving and active.

## 2. Fishing

Fishing is an excellent way to explore the outdoors and experience nature in an all-encompassing way. Many people choose to hike to their fishing spot, which can significantly help destress and relax them. Being out in the open of nature can be an incredible distraction from the stressors of daily life. This hobby is certainly not encouraged enough in young teens, especially girls. Fishing encourages individuals to familiarize themselves with local flora and fauna and get used to being out in the wilderness for fresh air, rather than being cooped up indoors.

## 3. Poker

Poker is a great way to boost your teen's concentration and observation skills. It encourages self-control as you ensure you are focused on your hand and has several cognitive benefits. It boosts mathematical skills and further develops logical thinking skills. It is an inclusive game yet is often treated as a game solely for males.

## 4. Woodworking

This is another hobby that encourages perseverance and focuses on creating a final product. It helps teens develop their fine motor skills and tactile side to create a project that they are proud of. If your child finds that they do not enjoy painting or pottery, consider enrolling them in woodworking activities to experience another activity that encourages creative thinking. It can be incredibly validating for your teen to say that they have made something by themselves.

## 5. Golf

Golf is often regarded as a male sport because it can be entirely male-dominated. But for a teen girl, this is a great sport that is challenging to master as it encourages bettering your own game. It relies on the individual developing their skill set to do better than they last did and can be a calming and relaxing activity.

### 6. Chess

Chess is a game that challenges a person's ability to think logically and plan. It teaches teens the basics of strategy by employing their observational and planning skills to make their move. These skills are also transferrable as they can be applied to life situations and social encounters.

### 7. Survival camp

These are a great summer experience for your teens to experience. Learning survival skills out in nature will teach teens lifelong skills that they otherwise will never be exposed to and in a controlled environment with instructors and peers. This is an excellent way to push the limits and test your teens' abilities against extreme adversity, alongside teamwork.

### 8. Music production

Get your teens to tap into their musical side and tie it in with their technical knowledge to express themselves by creating music. Music has many benefits to destress and help improve memory and mood.

## 9. Coding

For a long time, coding was a male-dominated field and continues to be in many ways. The gender gap does exist when it comes to coding. However, for teen girls, fostering this interest in technology and computer science can open up several career-wise pathways. Computer science is an important field that is rapidly expanding yet not enough girls are encouraged to pursue it as a career. Foster this interest from a young age.

## 10. Fencing

This sport teaches teens the dynamics of offence and defence while increasing coordination and agility. Another excellent way to promote cardiovascular health as fencing, while it may seem deceivingly simply, is a full-body workout that requires endurance and flexibility.

Ultimately, your teens' possibilities to pursue are endless, regardless of whether they are male or female. As a parent, it is crucial to rid ourselves of these notions that certain hobbies are "too manly" or "too feminine" for boys and girls. Rather than placing these limitations on teens, encourage them to pursue their interests wholeheartedly and dedicatedly. By doing so, you open them up to a world of endless possibilities that teaches them that there are no limits to what they can achieve.

A PERSONAL STORY

*P*arents worldwide have faced rough patches at some point or another with their children, no matter what gender they are. The teenage years are notorious for being particularly difficult for parents and children alike to manoeuvre. For Daniel and Lisa, parents of twins named Jessica and Jenny, parenting was seemingly a breeze until their daughters entered high school. They beat terrible twos and threes and got past kindergarten and elementary school without a hitch, much to the chagrin of their friends who were also parents but going through the opposite with their children. While they were struggling to get their children to focus on school and get over the separation anxiety of going to kindergarten, Jessica and Jenny seemed to be independent and confident and ready to tackle anything. Some might say it was because they were twins, and because of the constant companionship they had with each other allowed them to feel comfortable. Still, Daniel and Lisa chose to separate the twins in their classes very early to develop independently.

All of this went smoothly and just as expected. Feeling confident, when their daughters entered high school and began puberty, Daniel and Lisa were not expecting the problems that arose. They were undoubtedly unprepared to face everything that happened. This is often the first mistake that parents make when their children age. Being unprepared for the fact that your children are evolving and the transition from childhood to teenagerhood can happen in a blink of an eye that one day you'll find yourself faced with a teenager who talks back, pushes the boundaries more than before and knows how to get under your skin truly.

For the twins, this was a time of personal discovery and the beginnings of exploring their identity. High school meant newfound freedoms and pushing the boundary with their parents. But for Daniel and Lisa, they found themselves extremely uncomfortable and unable to handle the changes they were faced with.

Jessica and Jenny began experimenting with their looks, trying out extreme hairstyles and outfits. They were hanging out with a new cohort of friends as well. But perhaps the most worrying thing for Daniel and Lisa was the fact that Jessica and Jenny began arguing and quarrelling even more than usual. Their relationship seemed to diverge the longer they spent in high school, where the fights were intense and sometimes got physical. For the parents who had never seen anything like it, they were at a loss as to what to do and how to discipline their daughters.

Every day seemed more problematic than the last as it brought more challenges and issues that either parent, who were both working full-time, were unable to cope with. Everything seemed to come to an end one day, after a long day of work and school, when an argument erupted between Jessica and Jenny.

For the two of them, sharing a bedroom had recently become a point of contention that neither Daniel nor Lisa knew how to fix. The two of them had always shared a bedroom, and there was simply no option to separate them and give them their bedrooms. The argument became too heated such that Daniel and Lisa found themselves having to separate the twins when they began to get physical.

Having children who fight is a regular thing. All siblings bicker, fight, and argue, and parents generally tend to stay out of it because usually, it can be resolved between your children. After all, the issue may not be as severe. Daniel and Lisa's case was definitely on the more extreme side of things, but not an uncommon occurrence either. That is to say, having a hands-off approach is not by any means a bad thing when it comes to letting your kids solve their little arguments. Still, sometimes you might have to be a little bit more careful and stay on top of things and what exactly your kids are arguing about because the issue might be much more severe than you may have anticipated.

The good news is that there was a happy ending for the family, as they eventually figured out the twins' problems. Unfortunately, there was no simple cure that would automatically fix everything overnight. It took weeks and weeks of therapy and very serious and long conversations with all of the parties involved to get to the problem's root. For Jessica, Daniel and Lisa found that she struggled to find her high school identity and wanted to find her independence from being a twin sister, as she was always being compared to Jenny. And for Jenny, she struggled with the anxiety and hostility from her sister and didn't know how to cope with this, aside from continually antagonizing Jessica. The problems were complex and deeply rooted in both of them, and Daniel and Lisa finally understood that they had to approach them individually. There was simply no other option but to separate them and try to solve the problem by sitting each twin down and having a long and difficult conversation with them.

This is something that parents struggle with, and Daniel and Lisa were no exception. Understanding that your child is a person and having very mature and intense emotions is one of the first things to grapple with as you watch your child grow before your eyes. While not all parents will have a set of twins and the same circumstances, Jessica and Jenny's problems are by no means unique to them. Teens worldwide struggle with their mental health every day, and parents must stay proactive and involved in their children's' lives.

Perhaps the most helpful tip that Daniel and Lisa would want to impart onto other parents struggling to strike a balance in their parenting is to build a solid foundation early on in their kids' lives. The values that you instil in your children cannot be built overnight. This is something that has to be practised and preached from day one. You may ask how this helps with parenting teenagers? The fact is that this has everything to do with parenting your teen because this period in their lives is full of uncertainties that most teens resort to hiding from their parents. They lie and omit details for fear of punishment. Yet the crucial part from Daniel and Lisa's story is that even though it took a while, their daughters eventually came around and felt confident in their ability to share the details of their troubles with their parents so that they could seek help from them. From childhood, you should be implementing most of these tips to set you up for a solid foundation by the time they reach teenagerhood.

- Open communication lines: They say "honesty is the best policy". be open and honest with your children. This rule should be held to a high regard because lying to your kids will only backfire at some point. Not only that, but you are teaching them that deception and deceit are allowed. It's always important to differentiate between what you say out of necessity (for example, for safety) and lying with ill intent. This is crucial when it comes time for your child to open up to you. You will want your child to understand that being honest is a good and virtuous thing.

- Listen: While talking to your daughter is so important, knowing when to listen is equally just as crucial. As much as you will want to lecture your daughter while she expresses all of the mistakes she's made, carefully assess the situation to see if she has learned her lesson and go from there. If you recognize that she has internalized her mistakes and grown from it, take the time to listen carefully to what she is saying, rather than preparing your next lecture.
- Talk about *neutral* topics: As much as you want your child to be able to open up to you with their deepest, darkest secrets, remember that it's also important to talk about other aspects of life too, like what might be going on in their lives, how the school is, their passions and maybe even your desires also. Neither of you are robots, so it's important not to approach building a relationship robotically. Instead of being hyper-focused on the fact that you *want* to build a

relationship, focus on what you and your child are talking about.

- Create new memories: As much as having a daily routine with kids is very crucial, and sometimes you may not have the luxury to travel and do extravagant things, getting away and trying something new with your kids is so important. Making new memories does not have to be an exceptionally elaborate and expensive thing. It can be as simple as a ritual like Sunday brunches or going to the museum or even a movie night. These little things help build a strong foundation because it shows your child that you are first and foremost, interested in their lives, and you want to spend time with them.

- Encourage participation: Everyone in the family must practice these habits. By doing so with parents and all of your kids, this develops it into something automatic and done without prompting, which is precisely where these roots of trust begin. Your child opening up to you should never feel like a chore for them or you, so when it becomes an automatic thing that does not fill them

with dread and is simply a part of the day, you know you are doing something correctly.
- Share the load: Remember that it takes a village to raise children, so ensure that the whole family is involved in building that solid foundation. You might find that your attempts are not as successful as you like, but perhaps another parent, a grandparent or even an aunt might be having more luck with talking to your child. That is not to say that this is your chance to give up. Instead, this is your chance to try harder to understand what your child is going through and empathize with them even more.
- Make the most out of opportunities that present themselves: The car ride home is an excellent place to have a conversation with your child in a calm and non-threatening environment. Discuss topics that are easy and natural to both of you. Take these small windows of private time to get to know your teen.
- Take advantage of the environment: This tip goes hand in hand with the previous advice but a good time to have a conversation with your child is at nighttime. Bedtime should be

a calm and chilled out environment, thus making your child feel at ease and away from the stress of everyday life, which you might probably reflect as well. Building a calm environment can be difficult, so take note of times where you can simply just sit and relax and have a conversation with your child.

- Be brave: A surprising thing that many parents face is fear and indecisiveness in talking to their children. For many, it can seem like a daunting task. But the first step to overcoming this is not to see this as a task, but one of the joys that is part of parenting. Understanding that your child is also human and has their independent thoughts can lead to some very enlightening and exciting conversations if you let it happen.
- Stay committed: It can be an easy thing to do once and then forget all of these habits soon after. The truth is that you must implement these practices in your daily life and keep at it for the long run. This is how these values develop at a young age and stick around at crucial years like teenagerhood and when your kids reach the young adult age.

As much as parents might think that building a solid foundation is an easy thing to do, sometimes it can be far more challenging than you may have expected because life is incredibly unpredictable. You can never know what unexpected circumstances might keep you away from your child, and you never know what life may throw at you. As your children age, they get increasingly busy. Many parents end up struggling to find any time at all in their schedules or in their children's programs to sit down and talk to get to know each other, which can be so tricky when you want to understand your child as a human being truly. Bearing this in mind, it's crucial to find every opportunity you can to show your child that you love them and want to spend time with them. Your interest and enthusiasm itself can genuinely show your kids that it's not always about gifts or expensive vacations. For them, seeing your small efforts prove to be far more effective than anything else.

## TEENS IN THE WORLD

The scariest part for parents to come to terms with when their kids are teenagers is the fact that they are not around them 24/7, meaning their kids are spending increasing amounts outside of the house and more importantly, outside of parents' radar. This is the scariest part about your child growing and maturing into teenagerhood because for them. It means increased time outside of the home with a later curfew. For parents, this means more opportunities to get into trouble, to be in danger and be faced with temptations and the harsh realities of the world that you have fought so hard to shield and protect them from.

The first thing to understand is that your children are no longer blank slates. At some point, they have to experience the real world and all of the difficult things that come with it. Protecting your children from these things is essential, but completely neglecting to inform your kids about ugly things in life like abuse, terrorism, genocide, and some other scary but very real topics are merely setting your children up for a very rude awakening.

The fact is, as much as you want to protect them from all of the harsh realities of the world, doing so is just impossible because eventually, your child will have to face it all. Ultimately, you would much rather your children be able to handle all of these negative and scary things that the world presents.

However, what happens when your teen is just beginning to navigate through the world and is faced with alcohol and drugs? How does a parent prepare their children about the dangers that can potentially lead to even worse and harmful circumstances that might even affect the rest of their lives? This is a giant pill for parents to swallow, and a topic that many parents neglect entirely to breach because it can be incredibly intimidating for both parents and children. But it is essential. Not only for your children but perhaps their peers and friends as well, should your child have the courage to speak up when faced with a difficult decision like this.

The last chapter focused on building trust with your kids. This is the foundational basis for all of the parenting. No matter what, you must trust your children, and they must trust you. This is the only way to truly get your message across and for them to have the respect and thoughtfulness to listen to what you are saying and truly absorb the information. For many teens, things go in one ear and out the other, especially where their parents are concerned. But if you approach the subject as something incredibly serious, which it is, and convey that this needs their undivided attention, you are at a good starting point to have a serious sit-down about what your kids get up to when you are not around.

Ultimately, this is not an interrogation, so be sure not to treat it as such. Treat your child as the adult that they are about to be. Teenagerhood is all about recognizing and validating that your child is growing into their independence and finding their own in the world, so be sure to treat them as such. Once you have them in the right place to broach the subject, it can be as simple as asking them what they know about drugs and alcohol. Provided that you have the trust built between the two of you and you've followed some of the tips from Chapter 6, hopefully, your child will open up about the topic. Many teens will tread extra carefully for fear of punishment or discipline, even if they haven't dabbled in any of the substances.

Remember, this is not an interrogation. Be watchful of their mood changing or any guards going up. Perhaps your teen gets defensive. Remember that you are here to give them the advice and education they need, not dole out more punishments. This is where you acknowledge that they may have come in contact with substances and calmly educate them about why underage drinking and smoking are extremely dangerous and can seriously affect their health and their future should they get caught and even if they are not caught the bigger eye is watching.

For teens, drugs and alcohol are an exciting thing, mostly because it is so heavily frowned upon and beyond that, completely illegal. For many, the adrenaline rush of doing something wrong can get them going and making stupid decisions that will negatively impact their lives, should it go on a criminal record of some kind. This is why parents need to take an active role in educating their children and providing them with an out should they ever be caught in a position where they are too afraid to resist or say no.

Giving your teens a rundown of what they might encounter while they are not under adult supervision is a good idea. Teaching them how to spot drugs or alcohol is an excellent step to get them to steer clear of it and perhaps get out of the situation just in time.

There are multiple ways to approach this. You can tell your teen to call or text you, or perhaps a trusted older sibling/cousin/whatever the case is. As much as you want to give your teen the freedom to go out to that get-together, you also want to provide them with a way out that won't get them in trouble. It is crucial to tell your kids that they will not get in trouble for seeking help. Punishing your kids when they have found themselves in a sticky situation and have sought help is a sure way to make sure they will never make use of this exit ever again.

Practice lines with your teens to get them out of these situations, like coming up with excuses. These can be as simple as, "I have health issues" or "I can't come home under the influence, my parents will notice". It may take some practice but coming up with a realistic way can protect your teens from potential harm. And ultimately, for parents, the most important thing is that their children are safe and away from danger.

Trusting your teens to be on their own is a natural part of them growing up. The most important thing that you can do to make sure that they do not get into trouble is to educate them on how and why certain things are wrong and lead to severe consequences that even you, the parent, cannot protect them from. While you do not want to scare your teens and traumatize them from ever going out again, it is essential to teach them about finding the right friends who positively influence them and want the best for them, rather than being focused on ruining their futures. By instilling this early on, your child will be able to spot out manipulators and cheaters from their young age and will carry the lesson with them for the rest of their lives.

Focus on the fact that what they do when Mum and Dad are away are solely their responsibility. Instilling in your teens that actions can have incredibly grave consequences can be scary for them, but it is a reality that they have to face to grow and mature. This is merely another natural part of growing up and becoming a full-grown teenager, where you are faced with the not-so-nice realities of the world. Your teenagers are no longer children, and now, another set of rules, responsibilities and expectations are placed on them because growing older is not always fun and games.

Girls are more prone to be affected later in life by a past hurting memory. Whether it is effects of bullying, low self-esteem, mental health struggles or a combination of all of them, these issues will always return to haunt your daughter if left undealt with and untreated. It can create an incredibly dangerous circumstance for your daughter. Issues can leave a deep and permanent fissure on your daughter's personality. Mothers usually come in here to help their teen daughters face these issues by encouraging them to lean on their shoulder and share these burdens that are weighing heavily on their minds.

For Luna, her mother Diana was extremely perceptive over her child's switch in moods. She noticed almost immediately that her daughter was coming home from school subdued. Luna was not eating as much as she used to and was more recluse, spending increasing amounts of time alone and away from her friends. This was shocking for Diana, who was incredibly used to seeing her daughter surrounded by friends, and family. This was a clear indicator that her daughter was experiencing some difficult times.

In high school, girls tend to move in cliques and close-up units that keep secrets, which can be dangerous for innocent young girls. Diana felt like her role here was to discern what was bothering her daughter. Diana had to do some sleuthing that went behind Luna's back as she tried to figure out what was going on with her daughter through her friends. Word got back around to Luna, who was furious.

After a blowout argument that resulted in tears, Diana had the chance to calmly explain her side and show her daughter that she did what she had to do to figure out how to help her because she was so closed-off from her. Diana could express her most vulnerable feelings to her daughter, who finally saw that her mother truly just wanted to help her. Unlike the clique of girls at school who was only pretending to be her friend so that they could cheat off of her during tests, Diana was someone who would not merely get rid of her because she was bored or no longer useful to Luna. The blow on Luna's self-esteem was immense. But together with Diana, they were able to work through the bullies' negative comments to begin to mend and heal from the trauma slowly.

Years later, Luna would still have social anxieties that were rooted in her experiences from high school. It would scar her permanently, and social situations with groups of people became a new challenge she would have to tackle when entering the workforce. And Luna is by no means an exception to this. Plenty of people have experienced some trauma that was left unresolved from their childhood or teenage years. The difference here is that Luna was able to admit that she was struggling with her mother from a young age and work at it until she could cope healthily by the time she was an adult.

In some cases, girls may instead prefer to talk to their fathers than their mothers when facing difficulties. Regardless of who they choose, it is essential to develop trust between everyone involved.

Some tips for fathers raising daughters:

1. How you talk to and treat women will have a lasting impact on how your daughter perceives herself. Your daughter will be wise to the stereotypes and negative view you may

have on other women. Her identity is shaped by what it is to be a woman and growing up with a father who respects women shows her how to expect to be treated. Be positive and respectful. Avoid using foul language that puts down females.

2. Honesty and integrity in relationships are vital factors for a healthy and happy future. Demonstrate this to her to have a healthy relationship model to look to when examining her future relationships. Show her that just because her mum is not with you due to various reasons does not mean you will compromise the essential values. It also shows that you should be consistent with the qualities and values that are most important in your own life.

3. Include her. Fathers often feel like their daughters are not capable or too fragile to do "manly" things like play football. But the fact is that hobbies are not assigned by gender. Interests are simply that, just interests. So, involve your daughter in your favourite hobbies because she's only as capable as the next person. And before you

know it, she might even have a knack for it and do better than you.
4. Similarly, if your daughter wants to be girly, allow her to do so. You don't have to force her into dresses she does not like if she does not want to wear them, just because she is a girl. Allow her to express herself as freely as she wants without fear of being reprimanded. (This helps to know her way of thinking)
5. Don't avoid uncomfortable talks just because you are different genders. Ultimately, if the conversation is about biology, you just have to get it over with. It should never be a taboo subject or treated as such. Try your best to accept that this is reality and have an adult conversation with your daughter.

When it comes to helping your daughters develop and grow as individuals, mothers tend to relate as they may have undergone the same experiences growing up themselves. That is not to say, however, that mothers can be the only guide for daughters. This can vary depending on the individual. Perhaps an older sibling, an aunt or even a cousin might provide some guidance to someone who is lost or experiencing hardship. While Luna was lucky and had her mother to turn to, many people do not have that privilege and instead have to turn to other figures in their lives.

- Regardless of your relationship, here are some helpful tips for nurturing in teen girls.

Like the saying goes: "Like mother, like daughter". This tends to happen because mothers can only give what they are made of. Mothers can only share their own experiences to relate to their daughters, which usually ends up in many similarities shared between both mother and daughter.

- Love her and show her affirmations as a person.

Too often are girls' self-worth tied to things like beauty or grades. Instead of doing so, value the person she is on the inside and the good qualities that make her important, what she loves, and values. Rather than see her as lesser than because she is not a certain weight or wears a specific style of clothes, place higher importance on her mind, passions, and the type of person she emulates.

- Do not accuse or condemn her for her own decisions.

Never judge her for the choices she makes, even if they end up being mistakes. These serve as huge learning lessons for her that she will take with her for the rest of her life. These are also lessons that you might not be able to give her, and the only way for her to truly learn is by doing so on her own. Instead of being a voice of constant critique and criticism, empathize and be compassionate towards her plights and try to offer as much comfort as you possibly can.

- Be courteous and interested in her person and what concerns her.

Your daughter has her passions and interests that have shaped her into who she is. Her interests could be "manly" things like sports or video games, but that does not mean she should be limited from them just because of a societal perception. Respect her interests and take them as seriously as she would take them. Parents often make remarks that can cut deeper than they realize. Instead of doing this, remember to be respectful and treat your daughter as you would want others to treat her.

- Be considerate with her and discipline in love, rather than in anger.

Providing a clear explanation of what she has done wrong and how it could have negatively impacted her life is a point that is crucial to get across when dealing with a wayward teenager who is rebelling and continuously breaking the rules. Be firm and consistent with punishments and be sure to explain *why* she is facing the penalties. Fairness is fundamental to teens, and unfair punishment can lead to festering resentment towards authority. Your teen might be more tempted to rebel and evade any forms of control because no one treats them like an adult.

## "DECODING" YOUR TEENS AND HELPING THEM THRIVE

Thriving teens can be a more daunting task than a parent may have expected. As your teen is trying to find their way through the hustle and bustle of school, extracurriculars and friends, it can certainly be challenging to feel like they are growing and thriving as a person. For parents, here are some tips to help your teen ease into this new stage in life.

- Schooling: Stay on top of your teen's education. This can be an extremely volatile time that sees a lot of grades slipping. While marks aren't everything in life, they can undoubtedly indicate how your teen handles all of their responsibilities and newfound pressures that they suddenly have to deal with. If you have determined that your child is struggling with school, this may be the right time to find a tutor or take extra time with your teens if you help them with homework. The key is to show them that there is always room for improvement and how to work at something with discipline and patience to grasp a concept and excel at it genuinely.

- Talents: Your child is unique in every way and may have an exceptional mastery of their own. Whether its music or math, finding ways to truly nurture these talents and encourage your teen to find a passion or a hobby that they excel in is a great way to not only teach them how to spend their time productively, but it also shows them that investing in yourself is so vital to improving yourself. Here, show them that nurturing their talents is a worthwhile cause because it brings joy and educates them on new and unique things that exist in the world that they may not have been exposed to before.
- Sleep: Humans needs sleep to thrive as human beings. For teens, the temptation is to stay awake up until the wee hours of the

morning on their phone or computer. This can have long-lasting effects later on in life, not to mention severely affecting cognition and alertness during the daytime. Be sure to encourage your children to take advantage of sleep and perhaps even impose discipline over phone use if the addiction gets too overwhelming for both parents and teens alike. Furthermore, this is also an excellent chance to have a conversation about how texting and the lack of face-to-face contact might be severely hindering your child's interactions and socializing.

- Reading: Reading is one of the best hobbies because it continues to educate and entertain people worldwide. It is a great activity that gets your teens away from their phones and more importantly, can really exercise imagination, thinking, and even help with their mental health. There are plenty of great benefits to reading. The best part is that with a library card (which is usually free or priced at a low cost), your teen will have access to thousands of books and resources to expand their horizons. Giving your teens books to read will change their perspectives and

engage their brain into thinking in a more dynamic way.
- Enriching events: Throwing an event for your teen does not always have to be exorbitantly expensive, nor does it have to be incredibly complex and challenging to do. The important thing here to remember is that these events can significantly contribute to your teen's happiness. Making a day like a birthday or graduation into a simple event can motivate your teens and get them to approach ageing and to mature a little bit differently than simply just dreading it, as many do. Truly making someone happy on a day like this requires thoughtfulness, rather than an infinite amount of money and resources. Knowing your child and what they love is the key to making an event special for them.
- "Decoding" girls: The general approach for girls has been to decode them when this in and of itself is an inaccurate assessment for understanding girls. Girls and boys are equally just as complex, and it takes a lot of effort to truly get to know a person and understand their point of view and where

they are coming from. Regardless of their gender, every person is different and has gone through their own set of experiences. To truly get to know your child and help them thrive in this world, understand them as the individual that they are, rather than gender stereotypes.

- Empowerment: Parents struggle with empowering their kids and finding the right things to say. But when it comes to genuinely empowering your kids and teaching them how to see their full worth to reach their full potential, it lies in parents to be a coach and cheer them on. Once kids see their value through their parents' eyes and witness the fact that their parents will always have faith and believe in them, they will be able to feel empowered in their skin truly.

- Motivation: As much as you might believe in your kids' abilities, progress lies in their hands where they need to feel the pull of motivation and discipline to complete their tasks and put in the work and energy they need to give whatever it is they seek to excel at. For parents, while you are your child's biggest cheerleader, a lot of motivation lies in an individual's ability to come up with it themselves. Sometimes you might need to take a step back and give your teen some space to figure out what they are working towards and then guide them and provide the support they need. It takes a lot of balancing and trial and error to truly reach a point where you meet your child's needs and don't push the boundaries with overenthusiasm.

- Bonding: Developing a special bond with your child can help push them up and reach their fullest potential. While every case is different, daughters tend to gravitate towards their mothers, while sons tend to gravitate towards their fathers. Again, this is a vast generalization, and every family's specificities can completely differ from this. Regardless of your family's circumstances, having a close bond between a parent and a teen can genuinely make all the difference in motivating and empowering them. For girls, this tends to be an excellent opportunity to talk to Mom about body image and sexuality. The same goes for boys and their fathers. This can serve as an ideal outlet for your kids to vent and rant and come to you with any questions and concerns. Ultimately, it is genuinely based on you and your own family and the configuration of parents and children.

- Discipline: While your teens are starting to look like adults and might be coming into their own, they certainly may not act like it. This is where parents and discipline come in. Regardless of how you choose to discipline your teens, they will not be happy about it. When you encounter this case, it is essential to explain to your teens why they are faced with consequences. The appropriate disciplinary tactics for a teen usually revolve around taking away privileges like cellphone use or a shortened curfew.

- Focus: Focus goes hand in hand with motivation and empowerment, but one thing to note here is that having a compass when you are a teenager can be especially difficult because teens do not know what they want to do with their lives. Expecting teenagers to figure out a career focus and the rest of their trajectory for their education is a Herculean task. But this is where parents come in. Discussing things with your teens to help them figure out their future is one of the best things you can provide your teens with because this means honesty, endless advice, and constant reassurance that your teenager is never alone.

Lisa noticed her daughter Amy's personal life was getting increasingly attractive as she aged. By her teenage years, Lisa realized it was time to have a serious talk about relationships, and it was now or never. Lisa reminded herself that while some teens will start dating earlier than others, it's completely normal to have romantic interests during the teenage years. Amy was outspoken about her interests in dating while her friends tended to keep it to themselves. Regardless of how your teen perceives the subject, don't be afraid to begin a discussion because several vital topics need to be discussed and clear ground rules that Lisa had to set.

Lisa needed to coach her daughter on handling relationships, starting with her class friends. She provided some tips at the beginning that ended up being a gateway to open Amy up and continuously keep her Mum in the loop when there are new developments in her life. Lisa quickly explained to her daughter that relationships are a commitment and the importance of getting to know someone before committing to a relationship with them.

Lisa didn't allow her to lose sight of the important things, she was aware that relationships were not the end to life, but a lifestyle that makes her maker happy is essential. At one point, though, Amy reminded herself not to neglect other aspects of life like family and extracurriculars etc. But with Lisa checking in with her daughter regularly, Amy was able to see that other aspects of life were just as important that she had to give her energy towards. Lisa was always letting her daughter know that if she ever has any questions or concerns, she could always turn to her for support or advice.

One of the areas where Lisa saw that Amy was becoming too obsessed was with her technology usage. Once she began having more friends at school, Amy's usage increased by a ten-fold where Lisa previously thought it was not possible. Having more friends was an extremely new and exciting time for Amy, so she was enthusiastic about spending time with whoever calls her. Amy wanted to text and call almost every hour of every day. It took a serious discussion between Lisa and Amy on safe practices online and not compromising herself for others and being responsible for technology use.

One of the essential things that Lisa instilled was talk about consent, which she made a big deal because it is. Consent is so necessary at any age but especially when you are young. Lisa was able to articulate to her daughter that she did not have to do anything. She could say no. Amy understood how to set her terms in her friendships and boundaries while also acknowledging others' limitations. Lisa took the time to warn Amy of things that are simply unacceptable and red flags in relationships like signs of a person being manipulated, abused, or isolated from other friends and family.

Lisa was able to find opportunities to meet her daughter's friends. There is nothing wrong with wanting to know who your child is friends with, so Lisa made herself known to all her daughter's friends. If Amy was going out, Lisa was sure to ask where they would be going and curfew times. She got acquainted with all her friends, not only for her daughter's safety but also to show that she genuinely cared about the goings-on in her daughter's life.

While you want to stay on top of everything that is going on in your child's life, privacy is equally important. While Lisa was nervous about letting her daughter out with her friends, she trusted her daughter. She knew that she was responsible enough to do so because they were regularly communicating and keeping each other up to date. Despite the growing independence, Amy is still very young. However, Lisa gave her some privacy by avoiding the urge to listen in on phone calls or eavesdrop on them. You want to maintain a balance of keeping tabs on them without being too invasive.

Lastly, if your teen is going over to their friend's house, know who is at home at the other person's house. It was important for Lisa to find out who would be home, and she took it another step further by having a quick conversation with their parents about their rules and expectations for behaviour and conduct. These were all healthy measures. Lisa, as a parent took, which she felt was allowed to take to protect her daughter.

# RAISING DAUGHTERS

*A*s the other chapters have mentioned, you must see your children as the individuals they are, rather than stereotypes or generalizations that you might have heard. Daniel and Lisa from Chapter 6 learned this the hard way and found themselves faced with their family almost falling apart because they could not get their daughters to come together and figure out their problems.

So, there is no one size fits all rule that will automatically instil all of the best parenting tactics for you to grow your daughters with when it comes to raising daughters. It indeed does lie within you knowing your daughter emotionally and mentally.

This is a daunting task for parents, among many others, because how does one honestly go about getting to know their daughters and helping them grasp their internal and external identities?

One of the most significant pressures that parents face is knowing that they are always under surveillance by their children. But this is one of the most effective ways for your kids to understand how to carry themselves, particularly girls who will eventually become women. Seeing how Mom, in particular, handles herself and maintains her attitude is a guide for your daughters to do the same as they age and find themselves in various social situations.

Finding identity in a world of social media is incredibly difficult, especially for a young and impressionable mind like that of a teen girl. As a parent, it is crucial that you show your children how fake and artificial the online world can be and explain to her the sheer fact that most pictures have likely been altered and edited. Identity itself is a complicated thing that most women genuinely do not begin to even understand until adulthood. But when you are a teenager, you are forced to confront your identity quickly because the people around you want to understand you and relate to you. So for a teenage girl who is faced with the pressures of the people around her and the unrealistic standards of beauty that exist online, this can be detrimental and time and time again, this has been proven to be deadly.

Body dysmorphia and eating disorders are rampant in young girls today, and parents have to do their best to attempt even to begin to understand it and explain it to their daughters (and sons). Parents must use these formative years to instil a strong sense of self by reiterating that a person's worth is never based on their looks and adhering to beauty standards that are unrealistic and always subject to change.

Raising emotionally intelligent children is the best way to get your daughter to treat her body and mind healthily. The key to an emotionally intelligent child is teaching them how to handle negative emotions healthily. Showing kids from the minute you begin disciplining them how to recognize and deal with big feelings is the key to preventing misbehaviour — and this is a skill that will serve them their entire lives, especially when they hit teenagerhood and are faced with situations that they would never have anticipated. Being unable to handle emotions leads to more misbehaviour, trouble socially or even self-esteem problems.

The steps are simple: accept your child's feelings, and from there, it becomes a matter of guiding them through emotional moments and helping them find a solution to their problem. Sounds simple enough, right? The fact is that it can get more complicated than that. Especially when your kids become teenagers, and they disagree with most things that you say. Teenagerhood sees your child wanting to be more and more like an adult, which means ignoring all of your guidance and figuring out their path.

So what is a parent supposed to do in this situation? The best thing to do at this stage is to know where their boundaries lie and respect them. This does not mean that you have no voice in the situation; ultimately, you can choose to interject wherever you like. But the fact is that your teen will want to figure things out for themselves until they can no longer do so.

When it comes to tying in this newfound independence that your child is going through coupled with severe problems like self-esteem and self-image, finding the balance of respecting your teen's boundaries while also being concerned for their wellbeing can be extremely difficult. This is your chance to employ some of the essential tactics like listening and being a source of comfort for your kids as they try to make sense of what is going on with their bodies.

When it comes to a teen's self-esteem, focus on them as a whole person, rather than being hyper-focused on their appearance, leading to even more self-consciousness and self-loathing. There are some things you can let your child know that you are proud of; like her sense of humour, grades in school, or any other particular skill that is relevant to your child. This is also where the importance of finding fulfilment in hobbies and passions come into play. Praising your daughter for her abilities in her favourite sport, for example, is a healthier way to approach motivating and empowering her, rather than being so focused on a person's looks all of the time.

As has been mentioned previously, you are your child's most immediate and most significant role model. Developing confidence for your own body and showing that you feel positive about your own body will make it far easier for your teen to be optimistic about their own body. Having a positive attitude can be challenging to take on, but this also means avoiding things like fad or crash diets, making healthy eating and physical activity part of your everyday family life, appreciating your abilities that you are capable of with your body, having pride for yourself and extending this pride to other people and how you value them based on their qualities, rather than appearance. Be careful about subtle comments that might appear harmless but can genuinely affect someone. Commenting on someone's weight is never a good idea, whether the intent was right or not. Weight is an incredibly personal thing that every person has to struggle with. Making observations out loud is disrespectful but can also be difficult for a person to hear, especially since we can never honestly know everything a person is going through.

The best course of action is to have a serious conversation with your child about the changes they are experiencing with their body. However, many teenagers feel uncomfortable with this idea, even if you have built up a solid foundation for your relationship with your child. Sometimes the best course of action is to consult a therapist and see a professional to deal with these issues.

Teens are egomaniacs during this period, which means that you will be facing a lot of attitude and them even crossing the line in terms of behaviour. During this time, teens are hyper-focused on their problems and their desires. Teens may display selfish behaviour, but the critical thing to remember here is not to take any of it personally.

But just because bad behaviour is expected, it does not mean that this should go unpunished either. Teenagers can be extremely rude, obnoxious, and can cross the line into disrespect very quickly. They know how to push your buttons and rile you up. But as mentioned in the previous chapters, instead of getting into an argument or allowing your daughter to escalate the situation, just say, "You aren't allowed to speak to me like that. We can talk when you're going to be respectful." Perhaps taking away a privilege like their cellphone will teach them that bad behaviour has consequences. But the most important thing is for you to stay calm and remember that your teen will continue to test you and push the boundaries even further. The worst thing you can do in this situation is to give them the silent treatment or hold a grudge for too long because they are also susceptible during this time. Having an adult conversation is better than scaring them or arguing.

PLEASE LEAVE A 1-CLICK REVIEW!

I hope you enjoyed reading this book!

If you haven't done so yet, I would be incredibly thankful if you could take 60 seconds to write a brief review on Amazon or the platform of purchase , even if it's just a few sentences!

Your feedback will be a huge help in helping other readers benefit from the information in the book.

You can also contact us by sending an email to tcecpublishing@outlook.com

Like us on https://www.facebook.com/tcecpublishing/

Join our Facebook page https://www.facebook.com/groups/397683731371863/ to stay updated on our next releases!

See you there!

# CONCLUSION

While there are inherent biological differences between males and females, raising them lies in parents' hands to present them with all of the opportunity they can, regardless of gender. While society may insist on enforcing these strict gender norms, as the parent, you certainly do not have to and can instead choose to view your child as the unique individual they are and foster their personal preferences, hobbies and interests.

Always keep in mind to respect your children and their rights. Respecting their identity and evolution as they try to find themselves in this complex world can be a daunting thing for teens. It serves as another form of added stress, but when armed with their parents' support, the encouragement can genuinely build their self-confidence and love that they feel towards themselves.

While teen girls face a different set of challenges than teen boys, many of the techniques and methods of coping with this from a parent's point of view overlap and can be used interchangeably as there is no "one size fit all" approach raising kids. Understand that every child is unique, and it is a responsibility of the parents to recognize what makes their child different and act on it, instead of forcing them to conform to the status quo. This can be incredibly dangerous and force your children to close themselves off from parents to the point where you will have no idea about what they may be going through.

The cardinal rule that has been continuously reiterated throughout this series of books is that unconditional love should be the backbone of parenting. You should be able to strike a balance through trial and error of the different techniques offered in this book to find one that best suits your child to foster their development as an authoritative figure while also maintaining a strong foundation and bond with your kids that allows them to feel comfortable with sharing what may be going on in their lives.

# CONCLUSION | 119

Striking this balance is possibly the greatest challenge of raising kids. While teens can present a new series of challenges and frustrations, it is still important to note that raising your kids through this new stage of life can be incredibly validating and rewarding as you witness your children grow and mature into young adults who are trying to find their place in the world and make their impact. As these books consistently discuss the difficulties parents face when raising their kids, it is crucial to point out that raising children is an immense joy and a privilege that not all people get to experience, regardless of how desperately they may want to.

# OTHER BOOKS YOU'LL LOVE!

## CLICK ON THE BOOKS

[Link to Book](#)

# OTHER BOOKS YOU'LL LOVE!

## Link to Book

## Link to Book

[Link to Book](#)

[Link to Book](#)

## 124 | OTHER BOOKS YOU'LL LOVE!

[Link to Book](#)

[Link to Book](#)

# OTHER BOOKS YOU'LL LOVE! | 125

[Link to Book](#)

[Link to Book](#)

# OTHER BOOKS YOU'LL LOVE!

[Link to Book](#)

[Link to Book](#)

# OTHER BOOKS YOU'LL LOVE!

Link to Book

## 128 | OTHER BOOKS YOU'LL LOVE!

[Link to Book](#)

# REFERENCES

[1] https://cchp.ucsf.edu/sites/g/files/tkssra181/f/SelfEsteem_en0710.pdf

[2] https://www.theseus.fi/bitstream/handle/10024/50239/Anttila_Marianna_Saikkonen_Pinja.pdf

[3] https://ijcat.com/archives/volume5/issue2/ijcatr05021006.pdf

[4] https://www.harvey.k-state.edu/family-and-consumer-sciences/family_and_child_development/documents/CommunicatingwTeenTrust.pdf

[5] https://www.researchgate.net/publication/283721084_Early_Reading_Development

[6] https://www.understood.org/en/friends-feelings/empowering-your-child/building-on-strengths/download-hands-on-activity-to-identify-your-childs-strengths

[7] https://www.wfm.noaa.gov/pdfs/ParentingYourTeen_Handout1.pdf

[8] https://www.helpguide.org/articles/depression/parents-guide-to-teen-depression.htm?pdf=13027

[9] https://www2.ed.gov/parents/academic/help/adolescence/adolescence.pdf

[10] http://centerforchildwelfare.org/kb/prprouthome/Helping%20Your%20Children%20Navigate%20Their%20Teenage%20Years.pdf

[11] https://www.childrensmn.org/images/family_resource_pdf/027121.pdf

[12] https://educationnorthwest.org/sites/default/files/developing-empathy-in-children-and-youth.pdf

[13] http://drkateaubrey.com/wp-content/uploads/2016/02/Parenting-Your-Strong-Willed-Child.pdf

[14] https://www.researchgate.net/publication/263227023_Family_Time_Activities_and_Adolescents'_Emotional_Well-being

[15] https://parenting-ed.org/wp-content/themes/parenting-ed/files/handouts/communication-parent-to-child.pdf

[16] https://www.wikihow.mom/Trust-Your-Teenager

[17] https://www.statmodel.com/download/Meeus,%20vd%20Schoot,%20Klimstra%20&.pdf

[18] https://www.nap.edu/resource/19401/ProfKnowCompFINAL.pdf

[19] http://www.delmarlearning.com/companions/content/1418019224/AdditionalSupport/box11.1.pdf

[20] http://resources.beyondblue.org.au/prism/file?token=BL/1810_A

[21] https://exeter.anglican.org/wp-content/uploads/2014/11/Listening-to-children-leaflet_NCB.pdf

[22] https://www.researchgate.net/publication/312600262_Creative_Thinking_among_Preschool_Children

[23] https://www.gutenberg.org/files/15114/15114-pdf.pdf

[24] https://discovery.ucl.ac.uk/id/eprint/1522668/1/Thesis%20Moulton%20V%20281016.pdf

[25] https://www.bda.uk.com/foodfacts/healthyeatingchildren.pdf

[26] http://www.tuskmont.org/uploads/1/7/7/2/17728377/follow_the_child_trust_the_child.pdf

[27] https://www.apa.org/pi/families/resources/develop.pdf

[28] https://extension.colostate.edu/docs/pubs/consumer/10249.pdf

[29] https://www.empoweringparents.com/article/risky-teen-behavior-can-you-trust-your-child-again/

[30] http://www.wecf.eu/download/2018/05%20May/WSSPPublicationENPartC-MHMchapter.pdf

# PARENTING TEEN BOYS IN TODAY'S CHALLENGING WORLD

PROVEN METHODS FOR IMPROVING TEENAGERS BEHAVIOUR WITH WHOLE BRAIN TRAINING

INTRODUCTION

Parenting has undeniably evolved over the years. With social media and the rise of technology, these aspects have significantly impacted how we raise our children. We are exposed to new, creative, and unique ways to parent our children. These have had incredible benefits for parents worldwide as we navigate the challenges presented through parenting with a community of other parents for support and encouragement. However, on the downside, it offers some avenues for you to take as a parent to raise your child that can be overwhelming, confusing, and doubly daunting.

While there is no "one size fits all" approach to parenting, nor is there a single formula that will apply to every child, there are cardinal rules that are encouraged, especially throughout this book and its companion book explicitly geared towards raising teen girls. Along every stage within your child's life, one of the main cardinal rules is for you, the parent, to evolve alongside your children. You simply would not apply the same parenting techniques on a toddler onto your teenager, as much your teenager may sometimes test your patience as a toddler would. While your children mature and face new social situations and experience the myriad of new emotions that life presents them, they, in turn, experience personal growth of their own that parents have to grapple with quickly to develop their parenting techniques alongside them. This often poses a challenge for parents around the world because as much as parenting means adopting the role of a guide to steer your child through the various challenges that life presents, it also means going through a form of growth yourself, a notion that is quite often neglected when it comes to discussing parenting.

As an adult, growth is often overlooked because adults are seen as seemingly all-knowing and planned for the world ahead of them. Ultimately, growth and evolution are sure ways to develop as an adult and show your children that life is a never-ending series of tests of your strength and courage. Parents often fall into the trap of posing as an authoritative dictator-type figure in their child's life by being overly strict or adopting a "helicopter parent" style. Or the opposite can occur, where parents are simply too laid-back and hands-off when it comes to raising their children. Sometimes this can unintentional, or a consequence of parents attempting to navigate through the endless decisions they have to make for their kids. Many parents start this way, but the most crucial part is that they choose to evolve. They acknowledge the mistakes they are making and decide to grow and learn from them. This is the biggest lesson to take out of this book. You may apply the techniques and strategies presented in this book closely and strictly yet find that your child is not responding accordingly. The next step is to try another method and continue adapting and learning from this process. This is the single most generous tip that we can impart to parents: parenting is a process and takes time and growth.

Making mistakes while parenting will always happen as you attempt to raise your children to become good citizens. This is inevitable, and many parents grapple with this, even if their children are older and have been parenting for years. The fear of mistakes often holds parents back, which in turn can hinder your child's development. It is a complicated and scary feat for adults who have children, bearing this responsibility is no small task. Most parents are determined to raise their children to the best of their ability and present them with opportunities to grow and develop from fledgelings into fully-grown adults. With that intent, they are faced with the question of *how* exactly to go about this. This book is a response to this very question.

Seasoned parents would argue that teenagerhood is the most challenging time for parenting. Many parents might say that this period for your teenagers is a time of high emotions and added pressure as your teenager experience leaving their childhood and are on the cusp of adulthood. Your teens are in the process of making big decisions that will affect their futures, particularly with their educations and careers, which is an incredibly stressful time for most. Teens could be experiencing more complex relationships and the emotions associated with that. Additionally, as your children age, they become more accustomed to the fact that the world is more flawed than what they might have been used to during their protected childhood years that featured a far more idealistic and optimistic view. As your children age, they are met with the responsibilities they will have to take on as adults. With all of these in mind, the immense stress that can weigh on a teen's mental health during this time can be immense. With this age transition being so formative and crucial for your teens, the same stress and pressure reflect on parents, which is why teenagerhood is a tough time for both parents and children alike.

Yet these years also bring some new joys. As your children are now ageing, they are grasping a better understanding of adulthood which means that they can more accurately empathize with their parents and build a new facet to the parent and child dynamic as they form their own opinions and experience the world differently but can articulate and share their thoughts with you. This aspect is a joy for many parents, as they can develop a friendship and more profound respect for their children as they view them in the different light that maturity brings. Parents often find that they can share more with their children at this age, which is crucial for fostering a healthy relationship. Like most things, teenagerhood has its own set of positives and qualms for both parents and teens alike.

The most crucial point that will consistently be reiterated is that no two children are the same. Every child experiences their surrounding environment differently and has their notions of the world they are raised in. Likewise, all children perceive themselves differently, and parents must respect this. These books are framed through gender, with the first part catered to raising teen girls, while the second part is geared towards raising teen boys. Understand that gender stereotypes can be extremely harmful to children. There is no right way to "act like a boy" or "act like a girl". These are incredibly dangerous ideas that parents must avoid when raising their

Children because it fosters limitations on your children simply because of their gender. While there are rules that exist in society, what also exist simultaneously is fluidity. The concept of gender is a slippery slope. Still, it is ultimately up to parents to lay a firm groundwork and foundation to build confidence within their children to accept themselves despite societal expectations. It is up to dads and moms to teach their children that what they may like or dislike is simply due to their preferences and not a weakness.

For example, if your son dislikes sports, it does not make him any less of a boy, let alone a man.

The parts of this book are divided by gender to play on the multi-dimensionality that is gender roles. Gender roles are an incredibly complex and intricate social conceptualization as it deems a range of attributed and desirable behaviours based on a person's sex. This way of thinking can be dangerous and certainly place limitations on your children. As much as we discourage gender stereotyping, there are a few inherent differences between boys and girls that should be differentiated and discussed when raising girls and boys. However, keep in mind that all of the tips are interchangeable between genders and can be applied to any child as they have no prerequisites or preconditions that need to be followed before being used. These tips are universally applicable and serve to nurture your teen's interests and needs, regardless of gender.

After reading this guide, please feel free to leave a review based on your findings and how useful the guide was to you. I would be incredibly thankful if you could take 60 seconds to write a brief review Amazon or the platform of purchase, even if it's just a few sentences!

# TECHNIQUES TO UNDERSTAND YOUR TEENAGE SON

When raising teen boys and teen girls, there are some fundamental differences that exist. Some of these differences begin within the household, where boys are given less affection than their girl counterparts or allowing aggression and violent play by relying on the mantra of "boys will be boys". This is a slippery slope, as these notions that are seemingly innocent at the time can fester and develop into full psychological roadblocks that your children will have to face in their adulthood. These differences between genders are further fostered when your child enters the education system, particularly seen through the many education systems choose to segregate boys and girls during physical education classes. While education systems differ all around the world, the school system is often where these notions of gender and the applicable stereotypes are established with your child. By the time your child has entered their teen years, ideas of "running like a girl" or "acting like a boy" have firmly wormed their way into their mindset. It is an inevitable result of the education system.

What becomes key here is how parents pick up on what your child is learning and either nip these ideas in the bud or turn them into learning lessons for your children to show them a different scope that exists in the world. By doing so, you are setting your child up to be prepared for a world of diversity. You are also teaching them the incredibly important life lessons by imparting that they are simply not limited to the conditions of their gender.

Here are some techniques to employ to gather an understanding of how your teen boy may perceive themselves. This is the first step to deciphering how you might want to raise your teen boy and the techniques you want to employ to foster their interests.

**1. Have a strong foundation**

Having a relationship with your children is incredibly important and this is a known fact for every parent. A prerequisite to be able to even begin to help your children deal with the number of things they are facing through their teenage years is to have a strong foundation and a shared respect between each other. With the teen years being so divisive and stress filled, being able to face these challenges with parents by their side is incredibly crucial for teens. Similarly, knowing when your children are going through hard times or may be at crossroads really begins with a strong relationship that allows open communication and provides a safe space.

## 2. Be perceptive

Being proactive in your child's education and being aware of what they are being taught in their education is extremely important. For many parents, this may be a no-brainer, while some parents naively leave their children's education completely in the hands of their teachers. While teachers are incredibly vital and provide an insurmountable amount of support during your children's most formative years, playing a role in your child's education is equally just as important. Developing a relationship with your child's teacher and keeping tabs on where they are thriving academically can help greatly when it comes to tailoring your techniques of parenting towards them. Additionally, teachers are a great source for understanding how your teen may be doing socially and mentally, which in turn will provide next steps that may need to be taken in order to provide the support and help they need.

### 3. Be affectionate

Particularly in the case of boys, many parents make the mistake of feeding their daughters more affection than their sons for reasons in the realm of wanting to foster a sense of masculinity from a young age. This idea of affection and masculinity being tied is extremely problematic and can lead to plenty of issues down the line. Masculinity and affection are not tied together, and boys deserve as much love and affection that girls receive in their lifetime. Demonstrating warmth and affection to all your children equally, regardless of gender, allows them to do the same for their own children and avoid some of the issues that can arise out of not experiencing love from parental figures.

### 4. Avoid the "boys will be boys" mentality

This dangerous mentality is often used as an excuse to brush off certain behaviours or attitudes seen in boys. This is a slippery slope as it can foster violent tendencies and aggression that parents encourage as male behavior. It allows unconscious biases to form and allows boys to have a different framework of acceptable behaviours and attitudes that differs from girls. In other words, it gives them an excuse to engage in what could perhaps be inappropriate or unacceptable behaviour in the future. Using this phrase simply brushes off these impulses and is often used in specific cases of bullying which can be extremely harmful as it does not teach children that their actions are wrong and completely unacceptable. Instead, it gives them an excuse and a way out of facing real consequences and learning from their mistakes.

## 5. Be present

As much as your teenage son is growing up and becoming more and more mature every single day, while parents are expected to loosen the reins, it by no means entails completely abandoning parenting all together. You represent a guide for your child to follow and model after, even into their adult lives. Being present in their lives means continuing the relationship and bond you share, even if you may feel like they simply do not need you anymore. This is hardly ever the case when parents are evolving and growing alongside their children. Parents are able to simultaneously allow their children to flourish on their own terms while having a constant presence in their lives. This comes down to finding a balance and respecting the boundaries that your child imposes. While you may not like it at first, part of the process of being a parent is accepting hard to swallow pills like this and understanding that there will come a time where you will feel unwanted, but that certainly is not the case or the intention. What this really means is your children are growing up and becoming adults themselves.

## 6. Nurture self-expression

Limiting your sons to only express themselves within a framework of masculinity greatly hinders their development and can put your relationship with them in jeopardy. Rather than encouraging rigid binaries of masculinity and femininity, allow your children to gravitate towards their own likes and dislikes. These can manifest in a number of ways, from hobbies to the relationships they have. The important aspect of this is to always keep in mind to nurture these habits by showing your own support and respect towards your child's ways of self-expression, regardless of how it may manifest while you watch to know how to help. Every child grows and develops differently, so expecting your child to be just like your neighbour's son not only places unnecessary pressure on your son, but also sets yourself up for failure and disappointment. Rather than encouraging your child to emulate other people, allow your son to come into their own and become their own person. It largely lies on parents to foster this sense of self-confidence and respect of their own self. As your child ages, they will be more accustomed and open with who they are, and thus more willing to share with you what they are experiencing mentally, emotionally and socially as their parents.

## 7. Foster emotionality

Boys are often encouraged to not show their emotions, so much so that the stereotype is that girls are more emotional than boys. While this is a huge generalization, there is some truth to it and we may consider why this is the case. The reason for this lies in the fact that boys are simply told to put on a façade of rigidity and strength, where crying is now seen as a weakness. This, aside from being completely false, is dangerous as it encourages boys to bottle up their emotions which can lead to them spilling out in the most dangerous of situations. Rather than encourage your children to put on a brave face all the time, allow your boys to cry and experience the relief of dispelling their emotions in this way. Crying can be a healthier coping mechanism that can prevent your teens from turning to drugs or alcohol as a coping mechanism. The important part is to talk to your children after the fact and try to work out the extreme emotions they may be feeling. This has the greatest impact on your teens as they develop an understanding that their parents will always be a constant beacon of support.

**8. Be a guide**

Your children look to you as their role model from the minute they are brought into this world. This is simply what parenting is. But as they age, and especially by their teen years, inevitably your children will have more influences and face other figures who will greatly impact their lives. Respect this aspect, but also never relinquish your role as a guide to your children because ultimately you are still their parents. Always model behaviours that you yourself are proud of and respect because your children will model the same after you, whether consciously or not. Knowing that you have set your own standards for behaviours and attitudes in your household is a great way to find anomalies and notice how your child may be negatively influenced.

## 9. Family

The family dynamic can greatly benefit parenting your children because every person plays an important role in raising a teen. We have all heard of the African proverb "It takes a village to raise a child" and this certainly rings true when it comes to helping your children thrive and be the best that they can possibly be. Parents and siblings of an individual play their own roles in positively impacting an individual's life, so when it comes to understanding what your teen may be going through, relying on the different dynamics that may exist in your household is a way to ease some of the pressure a single parent may be experiencing. Siblings can tap into a different side of your struggling kid in a way that parents might not be able to. As much as the responsibility mainly lies on parents to bear the brunt of the weight when it comes to helping their children, there is also nothing wrong with relying on grand parents, the people around you to help out and play their role too.

## 10. Express how you feel

As your teens are older and more mature, they are able to relate to the emotions you may be feeling more so than they would have as a child. Being open and vulnerable to your children is an important factor to getting them to open up themselves. Rather than bottling your own emotions up, show your children that everyone faces extreme experiences as well and this will give them the opportunity to see that everyone also goes through things and they will therefore not feel as alone. While this is a way to show your children the realities that adults are faced with, it does not mean putting added pressure and burdening them with the problems that you are faced with. This is another means for your child to relate to you and therefore feel encouraged to share their own life more openly and willingly with you.

## 11. Professional help

Consider speaking to a professional if you find that you are unable to really grasp what your teen might be going through, whether it is because of reluctance on your teen's part to share or if the issue is more serious than you are able to help him manage. There is no shame in seeking professional help because it gives your teen a neutral party to speak to who provides a safe, judgement-free space for them to express themselves. This does not mean you are any less of a parent, in fact, it makes you a commendable one for recognizing your own strengths and weaknesses and ultimately placing your child's health over your own ego. Many parents struggle with the blow that their ego faces for they believe that speaking to a professional means that they are not a good parent. This is definitely not the case. Many teens recognize their parents' limitations and appreciate the degree of seriousness they treat their mental health.

Join other parents Raising Children | Facebook

The severity of what your child may be going through can vary in degrees. Ultimately, it is up to you to take the right steps and help them express their feelings and manage their emotions appropriately in a way that is sustainable and relieving. Mental health is crucial for a teen during this age, so take it incredibly seriously and be proactive in helping your teen.

# Your free gift!

AS A WAY OF SAYING THANK YOU
FOR
PURCHASING THIS BOOK, I AM
OFFERING YOU A FREE GIFT AT THE
END OF THE BOOK

## FOSTERING CREATIVITY

*P*lacing limitations on your teen boys on what they can or cannot do can be incredibly discouraging. Helping them find their passions can be one of the more exciting parts of parenting because as you are exposing your child to the possibilities of the world, they are learning a great deal about themselves and finding themselves. Hobbies are one of the best ways to do this. Traditionally, parents would limit their children in sports because of the idea of masculinity. However, as we have progressed as a society and continue to disregard these gendered ideas, it opens teen boys up to an endless world of new things to try to develop their creative and logical sides that can stay with them well-into their adulthood and for the rest of their lives. Fostering creativity for teen boys can often stump parents because they are still thinking in the framework of gender, where certain activities are exclusive to girls only. But when we rid this idea all together, we can see that there are plenty of options to foster creativity.

Some parents might question the need to foster creativity. Ultimately, it lies in the fact that as humans, we have some inclination towards creativity, expression and the arts. There are plenty of benefits to encourage your children to be creative and there are plenty. With TV and computer screens more commonly becoming the object of your kids' obsession during their teen years, fostering creativity is a great way to primarily, get them away from their reliance on video games and watching TV all day. Creative development is a great way to teach your children how to think outside of the box and problem solve. Teens are able to develop their reasoning and logic as well as formulate their own ideas independently without interference from teachers or their parents. Creativity opens up a whole world of possibilities for your children to explore in terms of art, dance, music, and many more. As children age, what can sometimes happen is that creativity is placed on the back burner as they face more intense curriculums in school. However, the need for creativity will most certainly come up during their adult life. Fostering divergent thinking from a young age will help them when they enter the workplace or higher education as they will be met with a multitude of challenges and hardship that will require thinking outside of the box. This is why it is crucial for parents to continue encouraging creative thinking and recognize the value of the benefits that arise out of this early on in your parenting journey and in your child's development.

Particularly for boys, creative development is often placed on the back burner because of the fact that physical education or mathematics and logic are instead deemed more acceptable for this gender. But as it has been reiterated, it lies within parents to recognize how this can really impede on your children's development. Placing them in boxes and labelling them and thus creating even more limitations only hinders them in the long run. So rather than raising boys to be masculine and encourage only "manly hobbies", choose to instead nurture their interests above all else.

A note about toxic masculinity: this is a social expectation that has been imposed on boys for centuries.

This essentially forces men into thinking that in order to be masculine, they must hide their emotions, be dominant and have a strong physique. This imagery is extremely dangerous for young and impressionable teens as they are constantly being bombarded with this idea of the "ideal man" through social media like Instagram. This pressure is counterproductive and can have a profoundly negative impact on how men view their self-worth and in turn view women and others around them. Having a conversation about toxic masculinity with your teen is a good way to educate your child about creating attainable goals that are realistic and beneficial for not only themselves, but for society as a whole. Toxic masculinity is a reason why certain hobbies are frowned upon for males and certainly why creativity is placed on the backburner when it comes to educating them.

The following is a list of hobbies that are often overlooked for boys or deemed "too girly". These are great activities to encourage your child's development.

**1. Theatre**

Theatre is an incredible platform to get your children to develop their self-confidence and public speaking skills. Acting, or even musical theatre can help uncover some untapped potential your teen may have. Theatre is also a social environment that many children thrive in as they are exposed to a cohort who provide support and friendship. Exposing your teen boys to new ways of communicating and is an effective and safe space to serve as an emotional outlet. Theatre is a good way to foster cooperation and another facet of responsibilities that your child may not necessarily have at home. It is another way to be a part of a team that is often overlooked, for "teams" often entail being part of sports, but theatre is another way to encourage experimentation and going out of their comfort zone while still in a group setting.

## 2. Stand-up comedy

Teenagerhood is a great time to foster this hobby. Not only does it encourage writing skills and independent thinking, it also places your teen in front of an audience. It's a great outlet to practicing communicative skills and a place to expel emotions in a way that gives them the satisfaction and immediate gratification of an audience. It is also a place where criticism is given freely, so it helps your teens grow a thicker skin and understand implementing changes and tweaking their routines to be better than the last. By the time your children are teenagers, it helps them While this hobby can seem out of the box, a number of drama schools and schools in general may feature courses or programs that you can enroll your children in to teach them the fundamentals of comedy for them to expand on.

## 3. Vlogging

The internet provides an infinite resource for your teen to develop themselves. Many teens have found success on YouTube as vloggers. Simply by sharing their daily lives and their journeys, teens are able to communicate and develop an understanding for an audience. Teens can also find their own niche of what they may want to share and develop their ideas in video format. This can teach them a slew of other skills from video editing to business management should they become successful and their popularity grows. It also encourages responsibility as your teens will have an audience to respond to.

## 4. Pottery

Pottery enables your teen to get to use their cognitive and tactile skills in order to produce creations. Through pottery, they are able to engage in a process that can help them concentrate and focus. Pottery is a quiet activity that can allow your teen time to destress and relax while also spending their time productively.

## 5. Dancing

With so many dance styles that exist, there is bound to be one that your teen son will enjoy. Dancing is especially beneficial because it gives your child another vantage point to understanding culture and learn about traditions and customs. It opens them to the world and its diversities and leads to empathy and respect for the differences that exist around us. In addition to this, it gives your teenage sons the physical activity that they may not be getting on a regular basis as they practice every day.

## 6. Skating

Whether your teen son chooses to skate professionally, competitively or recreationally, this is another way to get him moving and getting physical activity. It allows them to focus and express themselves through their body and movement. It promotes blood circulation and flexibility, things that are often overlooked for teens who are glued to their computer monitors constantly. Rather than being a violent sport, it encourages strength in a graceful way. Don't be fooled by how professionals make skating seem so effortless; it requires plenty of strength and discipline.

## 7. Gardening

This hobby is a good way to get your teen boys outside and getting in touch with their environment and nature around them. Learning about produce and flowers broadens your child's knowledge and exposes them to the world that exists outside. Gardening also involves being a nurturer, which is often not as emphasized for boys in the school curriculum or simply in their daily lives. It affords your teen son the responsibility of caring for another living thing while also allowing them to express their creativity by exploring the world beyond the confines of the inside.

## 8. Cooking

Similar to gardening, cooking is another way to foster creativity as your teen son learns their way around the kitchen and develops an understand for fruits, vegetables, seasonings and how they may all come together to create a final product that they can be proud of. This way, it also teaches sons that the kitchen is not a space that is exclusive to women only. Cooking is also an important life skill to have that your child should be prepared with as they mature and move on to the next stages of their lives.

## 9. Meditation/ Scripture reading

Meditation is a fantastic hobby to facilitate mental health in a positive and accepting environment. It's a great way to relax from the chaos of everyday life and to take a moment to breathe and focus on yourself, rather than everything going on around you. It also encourages self-reflection, which is always a good way to encourage positive thinking.

> *David found a secret which he shared to help all young people in the book of*
> *Psalm 119:9-11*
> *How can young people keep their lives pure?*
> *By obeying your commands.*
> *¹⁰ With all my heart I try to serve you; keep me from disobeying your commandments.*
> *¹¹ I keep your law in my heart, so that I will not sin against you.*
> *I John 2:14 says the same "I have written to you, young men, because you are strong, the word of God abides in you, and you have overcome the evil one." Keeping the word of God and obeying the instructions makes young people strong.*

**Singing**

Teen boys are often overlooked when it comes to pursuing singing. There are plenty of singing styles that will appeal to your son and their preferences and pique their interest. Many boys sing prior to puberty but feel the need to stop once their voices have changed. This certainly does not have to be the case. Through singing, they are able to explore interests in music and develop a deeper understand for theory and another facet of culture.

These hobbies have been featured here especially because of the stigma that surrounds them for teen boys who fear pursuing these hobbies. Your own kids may feel resistant to wanting to pursue these hobbies, and this is a great opportunity to discuss why and talk about the inherent biases that exist in our minds. Take the opportunity to explain to your teen boys that there is nothing wrong with wanting to pursue these hobbies, especially if they already have an interest in them and want to continue them but are afraid of criticism. Being a source of support and reassurance for your teen boys helps them build confidence and encourages them to pursue their interests wholeheartedly and dedicatedly.

Additionally, certain skills are often overlooked when it comes to raising boys as parents stick to stereotypes and adhere to gender roles and the so-called duties of each gender. This ends up setting your son up for failure as they will be unprepared for survival in the real world. There are a number of skills that many men are unfamiliar with because they were coddled and taught that they were the job of women.

- Basic household chores: both sons and daughters must have an understanding of how to run a household. Assigning housework and chores is not limited to women only. Doing dishes, laundry and other basic chores teaches sons to have basic cleanliness and responsibility over their environment.
- Basic cooking: being able to cook is a means of survival. Parents tend to assume that sons are simply disinterested in cooking and again, this can be a huge generalization. Teaching them the very basics is a way to prepare them for when they move out and gives them the ability to be more self-sufficient.
- Understanding the female body: plenty of men are still unsure of how the female body works, especially with periods, PMS and even pregnancy. While you don't have to get down to the nitty gritty of details, having a basic understanding of biology will help your

sons have a better understanding of the world in general. Plenty of males avoid this education because it is deemed to be not in their realm, but it is equally important to understand these things as it is to understand their own biological processes.

## HANDLING ANGER AS A PARENT

    *D*isciplining older children can be difficult for parents to face because it can be more complex than disciplining younger children. Because your children are older now, they expect an increased amount of independence and discipline from parents simply does not fall into that category. Many teens see their parents' discipline as a form of control or being overtly strict and not trusting them with the freedom that they think they might have deserved. So, when it comes down to it, your disciplining techniques might be met with reluctance and even rebellion. Teens will continuously test your patience and the limits of their independence while you attempt to strike the balance as they enter this new stage of adolescence.

As they experience new and extreme emotions from physical, emotional and social changes through puberty and aging, this time can be tumultuous for them. This is where you as the parent enter in order to help adolescents grapple with these big changes, and sometimes it might mean disciplining them and taking away their privileges in order for them to learn that there are consequences to their actions. Particularly during these formative years, serious mental health issues can emerge at this time. Most commonly, we see depression and anxiety manifesting as your teen goes to school and is faced with social interactions that can be negative. A deteriorating mental health can be attributed to a number of things and there never is one simple answer because it is so complex and difficult to come to terms with.

The techniques you use may take some getting used to as every teen is different and is growing up in varying environments. Ultimately, it lies on you to know your child and distinguish what will and will not be best for them, especially when it comes to imparting lessons. Adolescence is the time for parents to relinquish their reins on guiding their children and strike a good balance between giving them freedom while still guiding them through life. For many teens, this means less supervision, later curfews, or simply arguing with the decisions you may have made for them. Teens want to be able to do things in their own way and at their own time and being told what to do by authoritative figures like their parents or teachers is the antithesis to this. Teenagerhood also means breaking rules. Your teens may disagree with your decision to not allow them to go to a party and may sneak out or lie to get out of your rules.

From a parents' point of view, this time is especially difficult because it may seem like your child is doing everything in their power to test you and frustrate you. Teens are going to constantly push the envelope when it comes to rules and regulations and for you, the best way to cope with this is to remember that they will grow out of this phase. Stay calm and always remember to never act out of anger. As always, children are wired to mimic others and extreme responses like anger when you're frustrated can reflect in your children as well. That is not to say that you are not allowed to be angry. But managing your anger, frustration and stress in a healthy way is crucial for both you and your children.

The following are some tips for parents to healthily manage anger or frustration:

## 1. Breathe

Taking a few moments to pause and breath to process the situation. This is extremely important because it allows you to try and logically think things through; like how the situation may have escalated and how to bring it back to the point that is civil and respectful. But before you even begin to try and put pieces together in a situation that your child is involved in, take a second to just breathe in and out and count silently to ten. Getting into the right framework is important to thinking things through logically.

## 2. "This too shall pass"

Your children did not stay in their terrible twos forever. Likewise, this teenage rebellion will also eventually phase out, provided that you are supplying them with the right consequences and imparting them with lessons that they need to learn. In order to grow out of this phase and for this time of backtalking and disrespect to stop, you have to nip it in the bud early-on so that your teens can decipher right from wrong in terms of appropriate and acceptable behaviours and attitudes. Failure to do so will result in meltdowns in their adulthood that is most definitely inexcusable and out of question for acceptable adult behaviours.

## 3. Step away

Parents often send their children to their bedrooms for their children to reflect on their poor behaviour before having a talk with them. This strategy works because not only do kids get a chance at self-reflection, but so do adults. This is the time to think about what punishment your child will receive and the conversation that needs to be heard about curbing poor behaviour or attitudes.

## 4. Listen to your anger

Anger can often lead us to do things we might regret immediately. Rather than acting out of anger, approach your anger critically and try to think rationally. Sometimes your children may act in a way that is aggravating and frustrating that may warrant getting angry, especially if they endanger themselves or do things that you have explicitly told them not to do. However, in some cases, anger can form irrationally when your children do not deserve it. Rather than immediately acting on the anger that forms, consider why exactly you feel this way. For example, sometimes you might be taking your anger out on your kid after a long and stressful day at work. Your child is not your emotional punching bag, so always be wary of how you are responding to your emotions.

## 5. Avoid physical punishment

Spanking and slapping your children never teaches them anything constructive, aside from making them fear you. Hitting your children can have a profoundly negative impact on your child's development that can last throughout their lives. Being hurt by a parent completely destroys trust and a strong foundational basis. So while you may feel angry and frustrated, the answer is never to spank your children in your rage. It can render all of the positive things you have done as a parent completely useless because your child will grow to fear your punishment and find ways to work around it.

## 6. Assert authority

While your children should not fear you, they should definitely respect you as an authoritative figure in their lives. Reacting out of anger can often inspire threats that are unreasonable, which will in turn undermine your authority. Rather than immediately punishing them with threats that will not be followed through, take some time to think about an appropriate punishment that will make them learn and understand why they are being punished in the first place.

METHODS TO DISCIPLINE
TEEN BOYS

Once you have recognized that you are in a situation where your child will have to be disciplined, parents are often unsure of how to go about actually disciplining their teen boys. While these techniques are interchangeable and appropriate to be used on your teen girls as well, here are some actions for you to employ:

**1. Remove electronics**

Screen time is essential to most teenagers, with their cell phones, laptops, and TVs being readily available. In particular, cell phones are crucial for a teen's social life, with social media being a source of entertainment and fun. Restricting these privileges can get your message across to your teenager. By placing time limits, your teens will be compelled to reflect on their behaviour and encouraged to rethink their attitudes for the next time.

## 2. Restrict time with friends

Misbehaviour can manifest in many forms, and sometimes your children may not be acting alone. You absolutely can take away their right to see their friends for a while. By restricting them for a few days or cancelling a plan they might have had as a consequence, this will serve as a reminder for them to make better choices next time.

## 3. Tighten the rules

When your teen knowingly violates the rules you have laid out, this may be a way for them to convey that they cannot handle the new freedoms and independence that teenagerhood may bring. Giving them an earlier curfew might curb some of their inability to handle the newfound freedom that brings about recklessness and rebellion. Consider tightening the rules and changing them up to suit your child's development better.

## 4. Not all consequences will be imparted by you

Natural consequences can occur from certain situations, and they can provide an even better learning lesson for your kids. But it's essential to make sure the natural results will teach your teen something vital that they will hold onto. This is your chance to let your children be independent and allow them to face the natural consequences that occur from their actions. For example, teens quickly understand that forgoing their homework and studying will impede their chances of getting into a good college or university. Some choose to test this and push the envelope by neglecting these responsibilities. The natural consequence of this is that they will face a difficult time when it comes to applying to college because their grades are simply not up to par. As much as you want your children to succeed, sometimes they need to experience the consequences of taking their responsibilities seriously.

## 5. Provide logical consequences

Invent consequences that are directly tied to the poor decisions your teen chose to make. As they are older and feel more inclined to make their own decisions, creating consequences also benefits from preparing them for what is to come as they enter adulthood. For example, if your teen breaks something of value deliberately, make them pay to fix it. Or, if they are irresponsible with driving and the car, take away their driving privileges. These are logical and realistic consequences that will happen in the real world as well. They are not just limited to the household.

### 6. Assign extra responsibilities

Sometimes children need to earn back the privileges they may have gotten in the process of maturing. Take away their privileges and assign extra work for them to complete, like chores or helping out around the house to earn back the trust they have broken.

### 7. Be consistent

Mean what you say when you decide to discipline your child. Make the right decision on the best course of action, and the critical part is to stick with it, no matter how angry or upset your teen may be getting. Setting a pattern of consequences to your teen's poor behaviour and attitude will get through to them that all actions have immediate results that they will have to face.

## 8. Know your teen

Understand your teen's personality to figure out the healthiest and most effective consequences for your teens. Knowing what they are motivated by and the privileges that they treasure is a great place to start to determine the best course of action. This means that you must foster a strong relationship with them with open communication lines and judgment-free conversations. This is your chance to be more of a friend to your child as they divulge their details and share the things that may be bothering them or weighing down on them. Or on the flip side, they may tell you about the areas that they are thriving in. Mentally catalogue these things and keep up with the changes in their lives, unlike friends that come and go as these facts will come in handy when trying to parent your children.

## 9. Walk away

If you find that your teen is being disrespectful towards you and saying things that are extremely hurtful or overly argumentative, sometimes one of the best ways to curb this is simply to walk away. You may choose to say something like "Until you can speak to me like an adult, I won't be having this conversation with you." Then follow up with a privilege being taken away. This way, your child will have no one to argue with and will be forced to re-evaluate how they speak to you to regain their consequences. This is also the time to talk to them about how they externalize their anger. Speaking rudely to a parent is never the way for them to get their point across.

Disciplining your children can be a stressful and complicated aspect of raising kids that many parents dread but the reality is that it is necessary to teach them the appropriate way of life. Employ these tactics to try and teach them why good behaviour and attitudes in responding to the various situations that will arise in their lifetime. Teaching children to cope and manage from a young age is a valuable skill to have as it will follow them well into adulthood. While these consequences might seem exclusive to the parent and child dynamic, many parallels can be drawn when your children enter the real world.

# RAISING TEENS

*A*s much as punishments are essential for their development, there is a slew of other aspects that are also important to focus on whe n it comes to raising happy and healthy teenagers.

Focus on the positives to foster an encouraging environment for your teens. For adolescents, they are just trying to figure things out at their own pace and time. Parents and teachers encourage teens because they have experience in how the real world works and the world will not always tilt to their will or pace. As much as your child will make mistakes and test their boundaries, continually being on their case and punishing them for every mistake, they make sometimes might be a counterproductive approach. Instead, encourage and praise them by placing emphasis on the positive actions and why they were positive.

Set clear expectations for your teens to follow. Having wild and elaborate schemes only set them up for failure. With so many authoritative figures and rules to remember, the rules you set must be clear and concise so that your teens will see what is important to you. This is also a way to set them up to follow your rules if they are fair and straightforward. For example, expecting to be treated respectfully is a golden rule and a basic expectation that every child must be accustomed to. Communicate your expectations effectively and talk to your children about your feelings and desires. Let your teen son know what you expect from him and always explain why they understand your logic. For example, let your teens know that A's and B's are acceptable grades for you because anything lower will hinder their route to college. Or make completion of homework a prerequisite before they hang out with their friends. Consider putting your expectations in writing, email, or text it to him. This way, children will not be able to forget them as there will be a constant reminder.

Get and draw your teenagers to open up to you by avoiding "yes" or "no" answers. Instead, talk to them about where they are thriving in school and where they may be struggling. Rather than criticizing them for doing poorly, this is a chance to develop a plan to move forward to be successful on their next test on the exam. To establish a strong relationship with your teens as they spend an increasing amount of time away from home, regularly ask them how their education is going, who their new friends are. And how their quiet times, study time, extracurricular activities might be going. Setting time aside to talk to them about how things will help your teens grapple with the complex emotions they might be experiencing.

Whatever your household expectations are about relationships, this is the time to show your support for your children by encouraging them to discuss their lives. Parents find this aspect of their teens growing up incredibly uncomfortable, but it is usually better than for you to have assumptions about your teen, rather than not. This way, you can prepare them for what is out there and warn them about the dangers that exist.

Validate your children's' feelings by being an active listener. As much as communicating with them is important, listening is equally essential to be a good source of support for your kids. Offer them feedback and try to provide them with advice if they ask you for it. Validate how they are feeling and be specific when you acknowledge their feelings. It helps teens feel heard and understood because this period in their life being so volatile and complicated.

One of the enormous challenges parents face during this time is learning when to let go of their children and give them the independence they need to thrive and find their place in the world. The teenage years are crucial for this very reason. Not relinquishing control over your children can lead to disastrous effects as adolescents and parents will become at odds. Children will resent their parents for their over-controlling nature, while parents will continue to face frustration and disappointment because their child refuses to listen to them.

Finding that balance is the biggest tip that can be taken away from this book—understanding where your child thrives and where they fall short is how to build the foundational blocks to help them developmentally and socially. For parents, this is the biggest challenge because they seek to be a friend to their children while also being an authoritative figure that they respect.

When your children are young, you dictate every aspect of their lives; from what time they eat, what time they sleep, what they watch, etc. Teens are the exact opposite of this as they immediately feel able to handle the responsibilities that adulthood may bring and experience a surge of confidence in transitioning from the adolescent age group. This is the time where adolescents feel like they can control their destiny and make their own decisions.

Teenagerhood is a time for parents to recognize that this is where they need to allow their children to flourish independently. When kids reach adolescence, they need to prepare for adulthood on their terms, and parents have to foster this need to be independent to flourish. Attempting to dictate their lives by your schedule every day and controlling every part of their lives will eventually lead to them defying you the first chance they get and finding ways around your punishments and consequences.

This by no means entails that this is the parent's chance to relax and completely release their teens' attention or time. While parents are not the immediate influence on their children anymore, they still play a massive aspect in their lives as a constant source of stability and comfort as they are involved in their child's life. By shifting our focus onto our teens and letting them dictate the course of their lives, this means that your children will get a chance to make mistakes and learn some real-life lessons that need to be taught and not necessarily by you. Your job here is to provide them with the guidance and emotional support they need to overcome the challenges life presents.

Raising teenagers is not an easy thing because your kids will argue and have a differing view from you. Parents often feel helpless when they have especially argumentative kids as they feel like they're only not getting through to them. But ultimately, it is how you deal with these difficult times with your children that will have the most significant impact on them and will stay with them for the rest of their lives, so never rush when it comes to disciplining your children. Your influence now has to evolve along with your kids. Because they have this inherent need to be independent, merely telling them what to do can lead to even more arguments and strife between the parent and child dynamic. Some parents take this time to treat their children as adults instead of respecting their choices and finding the balance needed where you are still an authoritative figure that they seek guidance from. Talk to them like you would with other adults and do not sugar-coat things. Teens want to know they are in control of the situation, rather than feel lesser than and unable to make decisions for themselves.

As soon as puberty hits, a string of uncertainties and new developments will arise that your children might not respond well to. They may attempt to deal with changes personally and privately. Still, sometimes they may yearn for support from their parents to navigate through whatever they may be going through, whether mentally, physically, or socially. To provide the support that your child needs, you will have to discuss uncomfortable topics with them. This can be a too daunting task, but it is incredibly crucial to support your teens, especially boys. Boys are more often than not encouraged to keep their personal feelings and emotions bottled up than their female counterparts.

Featured below is a condensed list of important subjects to broach with your children, regardless of gender.

- Mental health: Prioritize your child's mental health just as you prioritize their physical

health. Boys are often told to bottle up their feelings and to curb this, start by having discussions about their feelings and what they may be experiencing. This is a way to show them that their feelings are valued and allowed. It also presents to them that you care for their mental wellbeing.
- Sexual activity: Teen years means engaging in relationships that can lead to sexual activity. While schools provide health education, make sure to reiterate to your teens with the talk. Be open and blunt with your teens about the dangers and temptations.
- Alcohol and drugs: Be open and blunt with your teens about the dangers and temptations of alcohol and drugs. You want to trust them to make the right decisions if they are ever faced with substances, especially when underage. Educating them on the dangers that these substances pose is incredibly crucial to making sure that they are well-informed when faced with challenging situations.
- Internet safety: Social media and the internet are a huge part of most teenagers' lives. It

plays a massive impact on moulding adolescence, and teens can often get so caught up on the latest internet trends. Impart on them safe procedures online, like withholding personal information and protecting their identity. Furthermore, it is important to reiterate that social media is too superficial. Social media can harm your child's self-esteem and confidence, so having a healthy relationship with Instagram, Facebook, and Twitter are essential to develop.

- Saying 'no': The word no is reiterated enough for teens. Educate your children on potential uncomfortable and dangerous threats that exist out in the world and provide them with a way out by letting them know that should they ever be in an awkward situation, you will always be there to support them and help them.

**Conversation with teenage boys**

With limited returns, contact with teenage boys always takes a significant effort. The monosyllable answers like ok.. no.. yeah.. dunno, whatever will frustrate the calmest parents. Those basic (non) answers will lead to further questions escalating to open up or offer more information to the boy. With a burst of hostility/anger, the teenager's system will react. With an expression of disdain or an audible tone of fear, they will counter.

An adolescent boy will engage in a whirlwind of extensive conversation on a matter of concern, amid the occasional lack of communication. Only pay attention. When they open up, don't discount them or ignore them. Otherwise, you will lose your reputation.

**The Moms**

When it comes to contact with a teenage child, less is better. A well-enunciated grunt may take the position of a long sentence. Mums need to know that attempting to describe things in depth is wasting their mental resources. An adolescent boy can hear just five or ten words. They shut down after that. Cut all correspondence down to one or two words, or even fewer mothers!

## The Father

To be a role model, teenage boys need a strong adult guy. Because of the loss of a parent in a boy's life, several youth harm reports exist. The human male has software that requires them to transform a child into an adult. This usually entails a passage rite set up by other adult males. For this rite of passage, a tutor, such as a father, may train the teenager. Much differently from most of the modern experience, our present world is made up. This programming does, however, still exist. Today, we are not handling this programming need sufficiently, which adds to today's social challenges.

Dad, Fathers or male role models need to walk their talk. Dads, first get your act together. Male role models need to pass on and show not tell, their knowledge of relationships, income, jobs, company, life, etc. Boys learn by doing rather than talking. Dads, making your sons understand how to be a guy is your responsibility.

Having a father who is worthy of emulation can set the life of a teenage boy straight. He will look forward to living a replica life of his father.

## Physical Task

Most teenage boys need to stay engaged. Testosterone expenditure and socialization would be allowed through participating in a sport or other physical activity. Boys want to be aggressive and challenge each other physically. Think about puppies or bear cubs. Playing fighting is a big part of their creation among teenage male animals.

Be alright with pressing and shoving people. Dads, let your son test you physically with boxing, football, mountain biking, etc. Don't just let them win," but balance their skill instead. Continual loss is going to be discouraging. They will deservedly defeat you at some point. A significant bonding tool for parents is adequate and regular physical interaction.

With their son, moms may also participate in physical activity. It is also okay to give a friendly bump to their sons while passing or a gentle punch. A welcome physical touch from any parent may be a back scratch or massage. Let them sense your presence.

For several boys, sitting in a chair is a struggle. There is a story about a teacher who taught his son to recite the verses while taking them on a jog to his male pupil, the Talmud. As they study, let them run. Maybe when on an exercise bike, they can read. This was a method used to engage his son's thinking while also participating in physical activity. While you may be inclined to feel discouraged that your son cannot pay attention quietly for long periods, choose to instead turn this into a positive by using it to everyone's advantage. In this case, the teacher decided to take his pupil's abilities and better his lessons that benefited both teacher and student. It ensured a more engaged pupil and a teacher who had a more pleasant time teaching.

**Be Robust**

Teenage boys will send out a torrent of nasty words in the face of a father, considering the frequent lack of communication skills. They'll appear to dislike you for a moment, and then wonder if the next moment is for dinner. They're not intimate, they're all hormones. Come on, mothers; you know that you can relate to a case like that.

**Be Competent**

Bear in mind that the adolescent years are also a time of research. Experimentation often entails dangerous activities. They can refrain from using sex, narcotics, beer, and tobacco. Before they have ample exposure to them, explore these topics freely with your son. This will raise the likelihood that when the time comes where they are faced with deciding on whether to consume alcohol or take drugs, they will behave responsibly. Establishing these ideals early on is not difficult. Parents often encounter problems because they have made these subjects taboo in the household. But the key is to establish open communication lines between everyone to instil the values you want your sons to emulate early on. If you teach your children from a young age that drugs are harmful, they will feel a stronger sense of responsibility because they can see the logic and reasoning behind these ideals. For your teenage boy, share family values and chat about what you think is right and wrong.

Have an attempt to consider your child's peers and the parents of their friends. Parent-to-parent contact can help create a healthy atmosphere for teens. Parents should help each other keep track of their teens' actions, without directing their activities individually to make them behave like little kids.

## Pleasant and Humor

Teenage boys enjoy laughing and having fun. To adults, the comedy could sound juvenile—well, it is. Let them be dumb. Whatever you hear teenage boys laugh at, you may cringe. Give them a brief reminder and move on to suitability.

Bear in mind that a hearty laugh may be a fitting solution to the unconscious response of a youth to a challenge from an adult. It doesn't always take a serious and dramatic reaction to let them know their negative reaction. A pleasant tickle and a joke can help quell bad feelings sometimes.

## Put yourself in their position

Pause to wonder where they are coming from as things start to go off course. Bear in mind that they have multiple thoughts, views, fears, wishes, etc. They will see the case differently than you will. Before things pass to the next step, get their insight. You may want them to wear new clothes. Be open to the truth of them having motivations of their own for wearing anything different. Stand your ground after you have listened to them. Be open to an agreement if the case permits versatility.

## Choose Your Fights

Parents and teenage boys are going to butt heads. Differentiating between critical concerns and minor issues is crucial. Urgent situations are those that would have a significant effect on your son or family. Minor complications are those that can present a temporary setback. Be firm on the critical problems and agile on the minor issues.

Talk it out when there is a disagreement. Get their own opinion. Share your view. Clarify all the pros and the cons. In other words, treat them while addressing the dilemma like an adult. When making a decision, be a dad.

## Set prospects

Children, in general, ought to have limits set. Teens, where there is opposition, would be able to have a more detailed statement. There is an intuition behind the opposition if the expectations are rational.

It is necessary to have them engage in the development of aspirations as teenage adults. Open dialogue and get their input on setting school grade criteria, actions, activities, etc. They are more likely to obey them as they help set the rules. Your teenage boy might believe he is on his own without fair expectations or you do not care as a father.

They will be vulnerable without this simple understanding of what to expect and will try to challenge you to see where in their world the actual limits are found. They ought to know who is in charge, what the rules are, and the repercussions of disobeying boys' rules to be happy.

**Value the Dignity of Your Teenage Boy**

It can be challenging for individual parents to embrace the idea of privacy for their children because they believe their company is everything their children do have. However, allowing some anonymity is crucial to making your teenage boy become an adolescent adult. If vital warning signs of trouble remain, then violating the privacy of your child is appropriate. Otherwise, backing off is a smart idea.

This suggests that your teenager's space, messages, e-mails, and phone calls should be confidential (Depending on the relationship built). Please don't presume that your son will share with you all his feelings or hobbies. Enable your son to place you on his friend's list for social media such as Facebook. This encourages parents to see what they're posting and doing to everyone in general.

For safety purposes, of course, you should still know where teenagers are heading, when they're going to come back, what they're doing, and with whom. Keep it general, not every aspect of their operation needs to be learned. The order would generate only resistance.

**Hold Your Confidence**

The teenage years, by extension, are just seven years long, between 13 and 19. You survived an infant crying through the night as a mom, the miserable twos, potty training, school, and another seven or so years of everyday trials and tribulations of infancy. Raising an adolescent can feel like a setback to your previous expertise in parenting. Instead, it is a test of your talents in adult school. You should not regard your teenage boy as a girl. Become his coach for adulthood, instead.

A PARENT'S SURVIVAL GUIDE TO
TEENAGE BOYS

When their' tweener' grows a foot taller and becomes uncommunicative and often explosive, parents are sometimes astonished. Welcome to a teenage boy's world.

Parents need to realize that through their progression to adulthood, this is a normal process boy go through. A fascinating, but the explosive combination is produced by the mix of testosterone running through their bloodstream and a natural desire to differentiate from their parents.

You look at your son, and you ask him to do a job. In a rage, he cries out. His poor language abilities stop him from being able to communicate his thoughts or describe them. You take this reaction as a personal assault and some kind of flaw in your son. Take a look back and slowly breathe. This condition has arisen since there were teenage boys on the first day.

The teenage boy is seen stereotypically as a wild, rebellious adolescent who is frequently in conflict with his parents. Although adolescent boys have their emotional ups and downs, they have a practical and compassionate side.

Developing freedom is the main force for adolescents. Informs that would frustrate kin, this is embodied. A boy who usually conforms to his parents' wishes will unexpectedly show himself and share his views. They strongly protest against the control of their parents and establish a moral code of their own.

Parents need to step back to realize that they need to build and create their own lives for teens (boys and girls). Do you listen to your adolescents as their feelings and ideas are expressed? Do you make it easy for them to have differing views and thoughts than yours? As you will for every other human, you ought to respect their opinions and viewpoints. For harmful or destructive wishes/thoughts, sound parental decision and interference are, of course, to be required.

**Handling Teenage Boys**

Parenting is demanding. None of the schools teaches how to rear children, nor do we have life models to follow. Otherwise, we will not have grandparents who spoil our teens because they believe they were not successful parents and so by their grand teenagers, would like to correct their errors; oblivious of our thoughts that they are overdoing it. Often the generational contrast of today from past generations makes it difficult to follow examples of life.

There is no question about it, and it can be challenging to raise teenagers; in reality, coping with teenagers is a feat with two parents, and dealing with teenagers is a struggle with only the wife. Regardless of how the single mother ended up becoming a single mother - death, divorce, and abandonment - she still has to play the father's role.

Plenty of parents, due to several circumstances, have had to become single parents out of necessity. Handling boys when you are a single parent and juggling all life stressors can be extremely challenging. Single parenting takes a considerable amount of courage and resourcefulness to play both roles of mother and father. The responsibilities are upped by a tenfold on the parent. Parenting can often be a thankless job that frustrates parents to no end. But at the same time, it can be an enriching experience to rear children.

For single parents, like most things, there is no one-stop-shop for raising children. It requires a tremendous amount of resilience and strength to face the journey of parenthood as an individual.

Maya is a single parent of three boys. The difficulties she faced were immense as she tried to figure out how to parent three sons while juggling her career and making ends meet. The most important tip that propelled her household into an organized space with all family members thriving was setting clear guidelines for behavioural standards. Maya understood that her sons were growing increasingly independent every day as they reached their teen years and saw that they needed guidance when facing crucial challenges that would impact their lives. For Maya, finding that balance was the most challenging part about being a single parent. But at the same time, it was not impossible. This took a lot of trial and error for her household to be as successful as it is today.

Furthermore, she involved her children in the major decisions that would impact the house. This is crucial.

Because your children are young, do not underestimate their opinions and treat them with the respect they deserve.

A crucial aspect of Maya's journey in parenthood with her three sons made her realize that there is no one size fits all approach to parenting. Every family is completely different, and no two circumstances can be the same. By accepting this, she could cater to parenting and manage her household to best suit her family. There is no quick-fix approach, or generic advice is available for how to treat your adolescents. To resolve the challenging challenge, any scenario needs a clear recommendation. But to help you navigate your teens, we will take those simple steps:

## 1. Set Laws

Your teens need to know the laws of your house and the repercussions of not adopting them. Make sure you negotiate this with them before deciding the rules and make adjustments if very necessary. You need to get their opinion on the laws that you want to follow. They are expected to have a buy-in to the rules. If possible, an understanding or majority must prevail.

## 2. Don't be too indulgent.

Do not be lenient now that you have a consensus. Laws are not produced to be ignored. They must accept the repercussions if they refuse to comply with your rules.

### 3. Give your teenagers period.

Financial difficulties are one of the significant obstacles of most single moms. While you are very concerned about earning a living for your families, you must not do away with time for your teens. During dinner, you will still find time to ask them about their day. This, in truth, is one of the rules you have to make. At a particular moment, the teens must be home, and you must share dinner.

### 4. Chat about crucial challenges for them.

Do not be ashamed to talk about drugs or underage sex. Your youth need to realize that in our culture you are mindful of these urgent challenges and that the goal is for them to resist temptations and social influences that will drive them to make the decision they will regret in the future.

## 5. Be careful of their mates

Guide them to select a good company. To know their peers and to make friends with their coworkers. You'd know who to call if complications arose. If your teens become secretive, you might even get details from their peers.

A story I would like to share features three brothers living together with their single mother, Janice. As a single parent, Janice figured out parenting her three sons through trial and error and found that the best way to motivate and discipline them was through a star system. The three brothers experienced difficulty for years, but as they aged, they developed endurance and perseverance. More importantly, Janice was able to impart a strong sense of independence within each of her sons that reflected in their habits as they were diligent and disciplined in cleaning up after themselves and following through with the roles they were designated within the household. Janice's star system entailed an inspection in their rooms and making sure they completed all of their tasks every week by Saturday morning, which awarded them a star sticker. Their duties included things like tidying their room, cleaning their clothes and shoes and helping her maintain a clean and tidy house. These stickers culminated to a prize by the end of the year.

On one particular inspection, Janice caught drink bottles underneath one of the brothers' beds. She scolded the boys for leaving a mess under their beds and compromising the standard they had held to a high regard for so long. She was reminded of a period when the boys realized the team effort that had to go into following all of the responsibilities and duties that were assigned to each of them individually. This was one of the biggest lessons that taught her sons to tolerate each other, persevere, and show each other patience as everything was a collective group effort. As all three sons shared a bedroom for their whole lives, they were all equally responsible for the messes they made. These skills and values they learned could not have been fully actualized if they had slept in separate rooms their whole lives. Sharing a room helped each of them learn how to look after themselves. The oldest brother exemplified the behaviour that was expected, which the younger siblings followed.

When parents and teachers understand a teen's point of view, this dramatically encourages them positively. The youngest son started to change when he had Miss

Helen as his English teacher. She became a positive figurehead in his life as she empowered him with her words of praise. She maintained a strong connection with him by deliberately investing in his interests. This grew an understanding for him as an individual, rather than other teachers at school merely seeing him as another student among a sea of many more. Miss Helen believed in him and his abilities, which completely changed his outlook. He conveyed to her that he was not lazy, but unmotivated because he was never in the right group of friends. She was able to see that certain activities bored him and made adjustments that suited him. Being an attentive and understanding teacher was one of the highlights of his education during this time.

The moral here is that parents and teachers can be huge role models for their kids and students. Adults have a significant impact on the way kids act and how they perceive themselves. It's up to adults to understand kids at a deeper level and treat them as their individuals. Too often do adults cast aside children because they might not completely understand the nuances that adulthood brings. But the reality is that kids are incredibly wise and often understand more than they let on.

The same goes for teens. A lot of teenage angst is rooted in them not being treated with the respect they deserve. Teens often get cast aside as hormonal and too emotional to be able to handle adult subjects. But this is far from the truth. Teens are far more knowledgeable than many people want to believe. Often, teens are perhaps more knowledgeable about the goings-on in the world than adults. The moral here is to take the time to get to know your teens on an individual level. Never allow them to stray isolated for too long because they may be struggling with something on a deeper level. Even if they are not struggling, seeing that they have a constant support system is sometimes very much needed.

With teenage self-esteem and enhancing their confidence. For teens, there are numerous and varied challenges, but taking the issue of self-esteem first.

About adolescents! Teenagers are trapped in an in-between environment. They're neither children nor grown-ups. They respond to physical and behavioural changes, including emotional extremes triggered in the brain's emotion-regulating portion by extra stimulation. AND hormones!

Needless to say, this is on the problem list for teens right up there! For many teenagers, this is a frustrating moment!

This time is hugely confusing for teenagers as they are met with new developments and are faced with their hormones changing. This can be extremely disturbing for parents, especially if they are unprepared to face their teens' unique attitude and behavioural changes.

This is mostly a time when parents might feel like they have lost control over their teens. You may feel like your role as a parent is redundant because your teens are acting increasingly like an adult. To put it simply, you may feel like your kids do not need you anymore. But because your teens are undergoing newfound independence and maturity into their young adult years, this can be a complicated thing for them to navigate alone, which is why it is so immensely crucial for parents to reiterate their role.

Losing control over your teens might come in some forms. You may feel like they are not listening to you or shutting you out of their lives. Your relationship with them might be hanging by a thread because they refuse to turn to you. This loss of control can be alarming for most parents.

Depending on the severity of the situation, you can do a few things to cope with this and try to fix the problem as quick as best as possible.

1. Find a neutral party. Something more significant might be affecting your teen deeply that they may not want to admit to you. Involving a neutral party that they trust like an aunt or uncle, teacher or seeking professional help from a therapist might be a route to pursue if you find that your attempts to reconnect with your child are not being met.
2. Be open with your teens and allow them to be honest without fear of consequences or punishment. This is when they will make a lot of mistakes, so allow them to do so.
3. Discipline them like an adult. The punishments you may have used when they were younger might not have the same effect as it would today. Be adaptable to their changes and act accordingly when you want to instil a lesson.

4. Rebuild respect. Sometimes resentment or anger might be festering, leading to your teen denying your role as the adult and the parent. If so, you might have to revisit your actions and reflect where you may have wronged your child in any way. This can be difficult to do, but very crucial if this is the case. In this instance, the goal is to rebuild respect between yourself and your teen so that they can grow to trust you once more.

5. Accept change. Sometimes you may feel like you are losing control over your teen, but the truth is that they are only growing up and experiencing the newfound privileges and perks of being older. The issue might not lay within your teen and instead be rooted in you not accepting the realities of change and evolution. If this is the case, you might have to reevaluate how you perceive your children because they are more than children and will soon become fully-fledged working members of society.

You may feel at this time that you are trying to rein in a wayward child, and all of the values and qualities you have attempted to instil over the years flying out of the window. But the importance here is to prioritize this child, rather than casting them aside and concentrating on children who seem to do everything right. Parents have to trust God that things will turn around. The critical thing is factoring in love with everything you do for your children, regardless of how old they are. Having compassion and empathy towards their struggles while also maintaining a constant love for them is crucial to come out on the other side of things more mature, secure and confident.

Teens also suffer, along with common confusion, from low self-esteem and peer pressure. Every teenager is susceptible to self-esteem issues. At this point, your teen's primary concerns are others' opinion, which can take a massive blow to their self-esteem. Teenagerhood introduces a lot of vulnerability that can lead to mental health issues manifesting now or later on in their lives. This is the best time for positive reinforcement because your teen is concerned with the perception that others have on them. This is when parents should be rejoicing in the positive developments that occur in their teen's life.

As parents and adults are concerned, it is our responsibility to encourage teenagers to promote positive self-esteem. It's an evolving process, and there are no shortcuts. It is essential to remind teens on an ongoing basis that they are amazing teenagers and that we are proud of them. Reminding them of their worth and value every day can boost their perceptions of themselves. But it is so much more than just telling them. Showcasing their worth to the entire family dynamic and why they are an essential puzzle piece gives them a better understanding of why they are so loved and cherished as people.

Adopt these tactics every day to increase the self-esteem and confidence of your teenagers:

**1. Set your teenager a good example.**

No matter how remote the teen can appear, the habits are very closely modelled. If they see that you have a problem with self-esteem, they can imitate that. Set a precedent of a positive attitude for yourself and others. Being a model of expected behaviour is a requirement from the moment your children are born. If you expect them to be polite, you have to be polite as well. This also carries into increasingly challenging and complex subjects like self-esteem as they age. But it is entirely necessary to be able to show your teens an excellent example to follow.

## 2. When seeking the ability to talk with your kids, lessen the time with teens.

Being able to differentiate when your teens want to speak to you or simply require your presence is an excellent skill to learn. It's up to you to understand your child's nuances to support them in the best way you possibly can. But if your teen changes their minds, they may not want to talk to you, make sure they know you're available. Sometimes, simply feeling that you're there for them makes a difference.

* Part of relating to a teenager is deliberately listening. Teens dealing with self-esteem sometimes believe that no one listens to them or cares about what they have to say. Show them you're listening by letting them finish and then answering questions about what they said. You might be inclined to give them advice as soon as you understand the issue given that you are an adult with more experience but resist this because the more important thing is to lend an ear to your child and allow them to express themselves to their full extent to get things off of their chest rather than bottling it up, which can do more harm than good.

## 3. Help set expectations for your child and cheer when they achieve them.

Start with small goals that they can achieve in a short period. Celebrate as they reach the target for them. Keep inspiring them if their target takes longer to complete, and their confidence will grow. A goal-setting mindset helps keep you focused on a bigger picture without getting too overwhelmed. Especially as a teen, ambitions can seem like a massive feat to try and tackle. This method is excellent to teach your teens how to manage their aspirations.

* Let your teen know that adjusting her aim along the way is all right. This is the way of life and an important ability that teens need to learn. When conditions change, we will need to re-adjust our plans. If your teen knows this, it will help build their faith. This is especially crucial because your teens will go through numerous phases and trends as they age into young adulthood. As they are trying to figure out their place in the world, what they may have enjoyed last week may not be relevant this week.

* Teach them that it is just as crucial to take definitive action to achieve their aim as to achieve the goal. Working hard is essential, and sometimes it isn't

emphasized enough. To achieve the goals that they have set, your teens have to accept that it will take effort and discipline to make a real impact. Warning them well-ahead of time and teaching them will set them up for a life that isn't full of disappointments and reality checks.

\* Failure at some point is inevitable, so be prepared to address these concerns if the time comes. Patience is crucial here because your teen may be experiencing even more self-doubt, disappointment, and sadness than usual. They may also be secretive of it. This is why it's crucial to have open communication lines that uplift, rather than condemn.

## 4. Let a teen son know that he makes you to be proud of him.

Tell them just how good they were when they scored an A. It's just as important that your teenager knows that if they get a C, you're still proud of that score. Encourage them to do their best and be proud of them as they do. Avoid tying their worth and value to frivolous things like grades or their appearance. This is a sure way to develop deeply rooted insecurities and follow them for the rest of their lives. Rather than doing so, focus on their qualities and abilities to constantly improve and evolve as a human being. This can be a challenge when as a society we are hyper-focused on determining a person's value through numbers or standards of beauty, but it does not mean that you cannot implement them in your household.

## 5. Encourage your kid to indulge in new experience they enjoy.

Being outgoing and open to new experiences is a great way to expand your son's horizons even further and expose them to new social, educational, and spiritual situations where they can learn and grow.

That could be any operation, gatherings, club, or organization. Getting them engaged in things would help them see they are more normal than they think they are!

Promote their individuality and interests by allowing them to choose the method. Give them the flexibility to express themselves by being involved in their desires and passions.

Self-expression is vital for teens because it serves as a healthy outlet when times get incredibly stressful or challenging. Encouraging your kid to pursue their interests prioritizes self-care in their own lives shows them that it's okay to take time for themselves and what they care about.

**6. Encourage your child to live a healthier lifestyle.**

Health is wealth, and encouraging this mindset is crucial for your teen to appreciate and care for their bodies to the best of their abilities.

If young adults are couch potatoes or have unhealthy food habits, problems may also present themselves. When a teen eats a healthy diet and needs a daily amount of exercise, it's easier for them to feel better about themselves. Childhood body dysmorphia is a genuine problem that can worsen during the teenage years. Binge eating, yo-yo dieting, anorexia, obesity and bulimia are every day during teenagerhood and can vary in degree from teenager to teenager. When adults don't prioritize health and demonstrate how important it is to care for your bodies, this reflects poorly on their children. It gives them unhealthy coping mechanisms and poor relationships rooted in abusing food. Meals become a time for managing their feelings, rather than dealing with their issues head-on and discussing the problems they face with a trusted adult. This can all be extremely dangerous for their health. It will take years of recovery to have a better relationship with their bodies if not dealt with accordingly right from the start. Meaning, it is critical that parents exemplify a healthy relationship with food. If parents face hardship with their bodies and food, it is essential to seek the proper help to demonstrate that it is acceptable to get help and guidance.

Arrange for a full check-up for your teen from the hospital. Your primary health care provider should rule out all physical causes for your teen's low self-esteem. They can also recommend more interventions or treatments that could improve the situation.

Set a routine for physical exercise in any form, whether its dance or a sport. Any movement at all is good and will help your teen live and lead a healthier and happier lifestyle.

Self-confidence can be low for teenagers. All the time you expend building, your teen's confidence can be torn down in one crappy afternoon. A small comment or bullying at school can exceptionally be a significant blow on a teen's self-esteem. Either can have varying degrees of severity on your child's perception of themselves. Something as severe as bullying is severe and needs to be dealt with. But the same effect can occur over a nonchalant comment that someone makes about your teen's appearances. Regardless of *how* it may have happened, it is essential to teach your teens healthy ways to cope with these comments. Leaving these unvisited can fester into more significant problems that will manifest later on in life. Having an open conversation with an adult they trust can exponentially improve how your child feels and how they internalize these comments.

There will be bad and great days for teens, just like everyone else. Never excuse or give up on them yourself. Try these strategies, and soon enough, you'll know you're on the right track. Your youth will go through mood swings, but they will emerge as a safe and stable adult with time and focus.

Talk about subjects with adolescents and teach them that learning to deal with rejection, critique, and challenges is a necessary life experience. Chat to your teen about how important it is to know that they are already a great person, worthy of love and attention, no matter what life might throw their way. As a parent, you are your child's cheerleader. Showing them that they are loved unconditionally, regardless of their looks or grades, is crucial to them tying their self-worth to the internal qualities they have.

One thing that is obvious about teenagers is that if they are happy and confident, they do better in all facets of their lives. Having a happy teen on your hands will reflect all other aspects of life, like school and social life. Your teen will have concrete building blocks that lead to a successful future. Adolescent self-esteem or lack of it will have a profoundly detrimental influence on the youth, so it's imperative to help your teen reflect on self-esteem and try to make it low on your teenage problem list!

Training and guiding your child is not forever, and you will notice your influence growing less and less as they tend to age. Since this is a time when they will learn the most in their lives, take advantage of this time to teach your kids to love and spread kindness wherever they go. Creating a solid foundation is rooted in encouraging them to live a healthy lifestyle. This will teach them to value their life, and the time they spend on Earth by doing meaningful things, pleasing their maker and leaving a positive impact upon others no matter where they go.

**Control challenges, rudeness, and ignorance**

Given that it is normal to feign confusion and refuse to engage in polite conversation during the teen years, how can parents connect successfully with teens to be understood?

This issue is where some of the most volatile arguments and rows can occur between parents and their children. Your teens will employ every trick in the book to get out of consequences and break the rules. Parents have seen it all, from lying to straight-up pretending to have not heard you. The excuses are relentless and can seriously weigh a parent down.

This is where parents need to develop healthy and helpful methods to deal with teens who resist authority. Instead of constantly arguing, try some of these different methods when it comes to dealing with your teens. The goal and most ideal outcome is to be as calm and collected as possible. Acting out of anger will only exacerbate the situation, and you will end up with a more difficult time on your hands.

Here's one way to deal with your teenager's lack of listening abilities: expect to hear you as they do. If you know that your teen has no hearing disorder and does not actually have earphones on and you speak simply in a vocabulary he also uses, assume that he can hear you. Look at him and clearly and calmly state your rules and expectations: "To get a ride in the morning, you must be back home by 9 pm tonight. I know the driving privilege is what you want, so make sure you make it home by 9." Here, the parent has carefully and outlined the terms. Nothing is confusing about this, which is an important detail when your teen tries to ignore the terms you have set, and you are in the midst of an argument. You never want to second guess the rules you have set yourself.

When he insists he didn't hear you when he wanders in at five past ten, instead of moaning about his hearing ability, you can say: "You know the rules. You didn't make it home by 9, but you didn't have a ride in the morning. You'll try tomorrow evening again. You've got the car in by nine the following day." Don't get dragged into a fight with him overpower. Turn around, and if he tries to pull you closer, leave the room.

See how that way works? Only as you sidestep the power struggle over touch forms, you can focus on the problem at hand and do what is right. Do what you can to be clear and direct even when referring to the back of your teenager's head when he stares at a cell phone page. Then, make him accountable for his choices. It's a conversation about a detour, and it won't get you where you need to go. Don't debate whether or not he heard you. Accountability is crucial here. Your teen might try to weasel out of a situation by making excuses and trying to transfer the blame onto something or someone else for fear of punishment. Your way around this is to always be clear in your standards and hold them to it, especially when they go against your explicit instructions.

If your teenager is routinely held responsible, it turns into your teen saying, "But I didn't hear you!" Next time, you could have a little discussion about paying attention and how he could listen differently. Know, you're going to understand everything if you keep your cool and stay focused.

Sometimes your teens have to be reminded that you are the adult, and that respect is a two-way street. In this instance, keeping your cool and not raising your voice is an example of that. As frustrated and stressed out as you may feel, avoid succumbing to these intense emotions because they often lead to even more rebellious and even explosive behaviour from your teens.

To make sure that the message comes out loud and simple, note these tips:

1. **Keep your reward before your eyes -** What's your goal? What's the only piece of information you want to get from your teenager? State your facts plainly and don't encourage your adolescent to drag you off track.
2. **Don't Take it Personally -** When your teenager ignores you, yells at you, or pretends not to hear you remember that he is attempting to be more powerful in this situation. Remind yourself that a power struggle or screaming war will only make things worse. Keep calm, even though you are annoyed, and tell the truth. If he intends to pull you near, turn around and leave. You don't have to attend whatever fight you're invited to. Keeping your cool shows your teen that being loud doesn't automatically exempt them from consequences. So, if you need to do so, take a moment to breathe and calm down instead of acting rashly and blindly from your emotions. Ultimately, it will only harm things even more by doing so.
3. **Don't be scared of the rules -** When your teen lobs a zinger at you to start an argument, hold the conversation focused on your

interests, not on your teen's thoughts about justice. When you argue with your teen on the rules, the irony is that it allows him to feel that the rules are changeable. Instead, stick to the truth: "I know that you disagree with the rules, and you would prefer not to listen to me. The irony is that the rules don't have to be liked; you only have to find a way to enforce them.

Know, remain cool, focus on the topic at hand, and encourage your teenager to knock you off the subject. Believe me. The teen knows that scratching his eyes, murmuring under his breath, and having a pessimistic mood makes you irritated. He's doing so on purpose. The more you demand the show of "active listening" (in other words, paying attention respectfully and acknowledging your demand), the more he will fight to ignore you. You're not going there. "Repeat this mantra: " Authority struggles are never a fruitful use of my time.

Regardless of age, your kids need to be met with resistance because it teaches them that ultimately there are consequences to all of our actions. If they are a toddler or a teen, parents need to adapt to this and apply the necessary measures to respect and obey the rules that exist within the household. Obedience can be difficult for teens and parents tend to cast these responsibilities to the father figure within the household. While there is nothing wrong with this inherently, this can affect how your teens perceive their fathers if discipline is always associated with him.

The best advice to curb this is by dividing up the responsibilities among both parents. This instils the idea that discipline is not associated with a single figure but is a universal expectation. While traditional roles would associate mothers with being nurturers and fathers as disciplinary figures, this can create a fissure between parents that carries over to children.

Regardless of how you choose to instil a sense of discipline and responsibility in your house, be sure to be mindful of how your teens receive the expectations. The best way parents have found to work around this is by involving their children insignificant decisions that will affect their lives. For example, while you have the ultimate final say in your teen's curfew, allowing them to negotiate and explain *why* they would like to spend time out later can be a good way for them to be more accepting of what they may see as your sanctions.

Additionally, if you are ever caught up in an argument about curfews, it would be an excellent time to remind them that everyone agreed the time set in the family. Negotiating and compromise are the best ways around difficult decisions. Ultimately, it's about reminding your kids that they have agreed to the terms, and they have to consent to the rules of the family that should be fair to everyone involved.

**Control challenges, rudeness, and ignorance**

Challenges will occur as you raise your children. This is inevitable. Your boundaries will continuously be tested, and you will face arguments and fights that will frustrate you. Maintaining a positive outlook can be a great challenge, but using positive language is incredibly important for your child's development, especially when dealing with sibling relationships. Parents struggle with this the most because sibling dynamics can be complicated and challenging to navigate through.

For parents, navigating through their children's dynamics is the root of a lot of household problems. Kids can be vicious, and for one set of parents, their son and daughter's relationship was too volatile to the point where they found no moment of peace in their household. Tom and Kelly were Will and Tiffany's parents and were at wits end when solving their kids' problems. They found that their older son Will and the younger daughter Tiffany could not come to terms with each other no matter what they did. They only seemed to be on relatively favourable terms on Christmas Day. The rest of the year was met with arguments, fighting, and tears from Tiffany because they argued about everything and anything. How did Tom and Kelly come to resolve the plight of their children? By following a lot of the tips and steps that are outlined in this chapter. Tom and Kelly had to regain control over their household and set strict rules in their home that had consequences for both of the siblings. They found that as parents, they had perhaps been too lenient with their kids, which led to disrespect behaviour and acting out from both of them. The best means of tackling this was limiting their kids' freedoms to understand that there are consequences to their poor behaviour. Tom and Kelly regained their confidence as parents and were able to set behavioural guidelines for their kids. While Tom and Kelly expected them to be old enough to know the difference between right and wrong, sometimes as parents you might have to go back to basics and essentially treat your teens like children again for them to see how ridiculous and out of line their behaviour is. Don't be afraid to discipline your children, no matter how old they get. Immediately, Tom and Kelly saw a change in their actions as they realized how childish and immature their arguments were affecting everyone in the household. For both parents and children, it was a wakeup call.

The focus is to train your sons during the most formative years of their lives to obey instruction and thus lay a solid foundation for them to thrive and evolve into human beings that have all of the good qualities. Letting a young and impressionable child have his way is a recipe for disaster as it leads to disobedience and developing the wrong building on the faulty foundation. Tom and Kelly found themselves in the face of education as well. Part of the root reasoning for the dysfunctionality within their family was that they could not decide on a parenting style that suited each parent. They finally arrived (after much trial and error) to the counsel they had received where fathers give explicit instruction or guidelines, and mothers teach by breaking fathers instructions into bite-size that is easy for the children to obey. Will and Tiffany's parents took the time to understand their relationship dynamics to help their household members. They were able to work together to break it down so the kids could obey. Fostering respect in a household is paramount, and doing so might not be an easy task when you have rebellious teenagers on your hands. Parents must teach their children to honour each other from a young age, and children must understand the social norm of speaking respectfully to parents throughout their lives.

## PLEASE LEAVE A 1-CLICK REVIEW!

I hope you enjoyed reading this book!

If you haven't done so yet, I would be incredibly thankful if you could take 60 seconds to write a brief review on Amazon or the platform of purchase , even if it's just a few sentences!

Your feedback will be a huge help in helping other readers benefit from the information in the book.

You can also contact us by sending an email to tcecpublishing@outlook.com

Like us on https://www.facebook.com/tcecpublishing/

Join our Facebook page https://www.facebook.com/groups/397683731371863/ to stay updated on our next releases!

See you there!

## CONCLUSION

Raising sons and daughters can be equally as challenging and fighting the gender roles assigned to them can be extremely difficult as your child enters the education system and faces various influences in their lives that will constantly reiterate these labels. However, establishing that your sons can flourish and respect their way of life is the first step to breaking down some of the societal expectations that are simply unrealistic and illogical. The fact that cooking has historically been deemed a "woman's job" is unrealistic in the twenty-first century and beyond. To raise self-sufficient and responsible sons, rid yourself of the inherent biases you may have and focus on wholeheartedly bringing up your teen sons to succeed in their lives in whatever way they choose to do so. Instead of encouraging them to follow the status quo, provide them with the tools they need to nurture their likes and dislikes.

Teen boys are faced with their own set of identity-related issues as they grapple with the framework of masculinity that is imposed on them. Some boys choose to act within this framework, while others choose not.

Parents are to pray for them, encourage and guide them with their decisions and be their cheerleader. Help them nurture their instincts, follow the leading of their conscience, which gets more sensitive as they read and follow the scriptures.

Young people have so much untapped potential that society will end up stifling because of the strict norms that are continuously enforced through its institutions like schools and the workforce. These highly gendered environments emphasize traditional male and female stereotypes which greatly limit teens all together. It can have a severe effect on a person's well-being and hinder confidence. However, this can all be controlled and completely disregarded in the household, where parents can control the message they want to send out to their children. Rather than focusing on these traditional stereotypes, choosing to instead foster true-love and confidence in your abilities is an excellent way to teach your children that it is perfectly acceptable to be themselves, no matter what society may tell them.

Toxic masculinity can subconsciously worm its way into your teen's consciousness through social media or even their peers and the interactions that they have. Establishing early on that this is a harmful way of thinking can save your teenage son a lot of grief and hardship as they grapple with their identity in the process of maturing and ageing. Establish that they are not defined by society's harmful standards of

masculinity and encourage them to develop their own identity that they are comfortable with and proud of from their maker's perspective, which is known more when they read the scriptures...

The challenge comes in at the vital part of successfully raising sons (and children in general), which is to strike a balance between allowing them to express themselves freely and disciplining them should they cross the line. It is a complicated task that many parents find daunting and at times, impossible to do. But now, armed with the tips and techniques of these books, you will be able to find that balance in your household to raise sons that follow the appropriate conventions of life while also flourishing in their own space.

While this book discusses disciplining teens and how parents can be extremely frustrated or angered by behaviours, it is also crucial to note how parenting itself is an incredible privilege and a joy as you watch your teens grow and develop. Parents can see the pieces of knowledge that they imparted on their kids from a young age come out when they are older, and the pride associated with your child growing up to be good people is indescribable. Disciplining your children can seem like a dreaded thing, but it is merely one of the many facets that are part of being a parent. There are always going to be upsides and downsides to everything.

Parents need to realize that this is a normal process boys go through, through their adulthood progression. A fascinating, but the explosive combination is produced by the mix of testosterone running through their bloodstream and a natural desire to differentiate from their parents.

You look at your son, and you ask him to do a job. In a rage, he cries out. His poor language abilities stop him from being able to communicate his thoughts or describe them. You take this reaction as a personal assault and some kind of flaw in your son. Take a look back and slowly breathe. This condition has arisen since there were teenage boys on the first day.

The teenage boy is seen stereotypically as a wild, rebellious adolescent who is always in conflict with his parents. Although adolescent boys have their emotional ups and downs, they have a practical and compassionate side.

Developing freedom is the main force for adolescents. Informs that would frustrate kin, this is embodied. A boy who usually conforms to his parents' wishes will unexpectedly show himself and share his views. They strongly protest against the control of their parents and establish a moral code of their own.

Parents need to step back to realize that they need to build and create their own lives for teens (boys and girls). Do you listen to your kids as their feelings and ideas are expressed? Do you make it easy for them to have differing views and thoughts than yours? As you will for every other human, you ought to respect their opinions and viewpoints. For harmful or destructive wishes/thoughts, sound parental decision and interference are, of course, to be required.

Other Books You'll Love!

OTHER BOOKS YOU'LL LOVE!

CLICK ON THE BOOKS

Link to Book

# OTHER BOOKS YOU'LL LOVE!

[Link to Book](#)

[Link to Book](#)

# OTHER BOOKS YOU'LL LOVE! | 243

[Link to Book](#)

[Link to Book](#)

## 244 | OTHER BOOKS YOU'LL LOVE!

Link to Book

Link to Book

## OTHER BOOKS YOU'LL LOVE! | 245

[Link to Book](#)

[Link to Book](#)

## 246 | OTHER BOOKS YOU'LL LOVE!

[Link to Book](#)

[Link to Book](#)

## OTHER BOOKS YOU'LL LOVE! | 247

[Link to Book](#)

## OTHER BOOKS YOU'LL LOVE!

[Link to Book](#)

# Your free gift!

**DOWNLOAD
YOUR FREE COPY
HERE**

REFERENCES

[1] https://cchp.ucsf.edu/sites/g/files/tkssra181/f/SelfEsteem_en0710.pdf

[2] https://www.theseus.fi/bitstream/handle/10024/50239/Anttila_Marianna_Saikkonen_Pinja.pdf

[3] https://ijcat.com/archives/volume5/issue2/ijcatr05021006.pdf

[4] https://www.harvey.k-state.edu/family-and-consumer-sciences/family_and_child_development/documents/CommunicatingwTeenTrust.pdf

[5] https://www.researchgate.net/publication/283721084_Early_Reading_Development

[6] https://www.understood.org/en/friends-feelings/empowering-your-child/building-on-strengths/download-hands-on-activity-to-identify-your-childs-strengths

[7] https://www.wfm.noaa.gov/pdfs/ParentingYourTeen_Handout1.pdf

[8] https://www.helpguide.org/articles/depression/parents-guide-to-teen-depression.htm?pdf=13027

[9] https://www2.ed.gov/parents/academic/help/adolescence/adolescence.pdf

[10] http://centerforchildwelfare.org/kb/prprouthome/Helping%20Your%20Children%20Navigate%20Their%20Teenage%20Years.pdf

[11] https://www.childrensmn.org/images/family_resource_pdf/027121.pdf

[12] https://educationnorthwest.org/sites/default/files/developing-empathy-in-children-and-youth.pdf

[13] http://drkateaubrey.com/wp-content/uploads/2016/02/Parenting-Your-Strong-Willed-Child.pdf

[14] https://www.researchgate.net/publication/263227023_Family_Time_Activities_and_Adolescents'_Emotional_Well-being

[15] https://parenting-ed.org/wp-content/themes/parenting-ed/files/handouts/communication-parent-to-child.pdf

[16] https://www.wikihow.mom/Trust-Your-Teenager

[17] https://www.statmodel.com/download/Meeus,%20vd%20Schoot,%20Klimstra%20&.pdf

[18] https://www.nap.edu/resource/19401/ProfKnowCompFINAL.pdf

[19] http://www.delmarlearning.com/companions/content/1418019224/AdditionalSupport/box11.1.pdf

[20] http://resources.beyondblue.org.au/prism/file?token=BL/1810_A

[21] https://exeter.anglican.org/wp-content/uploads/2014/11/Listening-to-children-leaflet_NCB.pdf

[22] https://www.researchgate.net/publication/312600262_Creative_Thinking_among_Preschool_Children

[23] https://www.gutenberg.org/files/15114/15114-pdf.pdf

[24] https://discovery.ucl.ac.uk/id/eprint/1522668/1/Thesis%20Moulton%20V%20281016.pdf

[25] https://www.bda.uk.com/foodfacts/healthyeatingchildren.pdf

[26] http://www.tuskmont.org/uploads/1/7/7/2/17728377/follow_the_child_trust_the_child.pdf

[27] https://www.apa.org/pi/families/resources/develop.pdf

[28] https://extension.colostate.edu/docs/pubs/consumer/10249.pdf

[29] https://www.empoweringparents.com/article/risky-teen-behavior-can-you-trust-your-child-again/

[30] http://www.wecf.eu/download/2018/05%20May/WSSPPublicationENPartC-MHMchapter.pdf

OTHER BOOKS YOU'LL LOVE!

CLICK ON THE BOOKS

Link to Book

## 256 | OTHER BOOKS YOU'LL LOVE!

[Link to Book](#)

[Link to Book](#)

## OTHER BOOKS YOU'LL LOVE! | 257

[Link to Book](#)

[Link to Book](#)

## 258 | OTHER BOOKS YOU'LL LOVE!

Link to Book

Link to Book

Link to Book

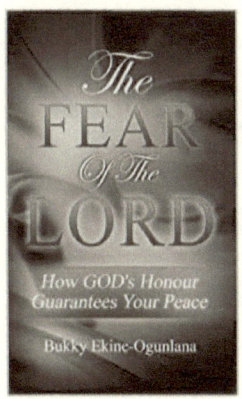

Link to Book

## 260 | OTHER BOOKS YOU'LL LOVE!

Link to Book

Link to Book

[Link to Book](#)

# OTHER BOOKS YOU'LL LOVE!

[Link to Book](#)

REFERENCES

[1] https://cchp.ucsf.edu/sites/g/files/tkssra181/f/SelfEsteem_en0710.pdf

[2] https://www.theseus.fi/bitstream/handle/10024/50239/Anttila_Marianna_Saikkonen_Pinja.pdf

[3] https://ijcat.com/archives/volume5/issue2/ijcatr05021006.pdf

[4] https://www.harvey.k-state.edu/family-and-consumer-sciences/family_and_child_development/documents/CommunicatingwTeenTrust.pdf

[5] https://www.researchgate.net/publication/283721084_Early_Reading_Development

[6] https://www.understood.org/en/friends-feelings/empowering-your-child/building-on-strengths/download-hands-on-activity-to-identify-your-childs-strengths

[7] https://www.wfm.noaa.gov/pdfs/ParentingYourTeen_Handout1.pdf

[8] https://www.helpguide.org/articles/depression/parents-guide-to-teen-depression.htm?pdf=13027

[9] https://www2.ed.gov/parents/academic/help/adolescence/adolescence.pdf

[10] http://centerforchildwelfare.org/kb/prprouthome/Helping%20Your%20Children%20Navigate%20Their%20Teenage%20Years.pdf

[11] https://www.childrensmn.org/images/family_resource_pdf/027121.pdf

[12] https://educationnorthwest.org/sites/default/files/developing-empathy-in-children-and-youth.pdf

[13] http://drkateaubrey.com/wp-content/uploads/2016/02/Parenting-Your-Strong-Willed-Child.pdf

[14] https://www.researchgate.net/publication/263227023_Family_Time_Activities_and_Adolescents'_Emotional_Well-being

[15] https://parenting-ed.org/wp-content/themes/parenting-ed/files/handouts/communication-parent-to-child.pdf

[16] https://www.wikihow.mom/Trust-Your-Teenager

[17] https://www.statmodel.com/download/Meeus,%20vd%20Schoot,%20Klimstra%20&.pdf

[18] https://www.nap.edu/resource/19401/ProfKnowCompFINAL.pdf

[19] http://www.delmarlearning.com/companions/content/1418019224/AdditionalSupport/box11.1.pdf

[20] http://resources.beyondblue.org.au/prism/file?token=BL/1810_A

[21] https://exeter.anglican.org/wp-content/uploads/2014/11/Listening-to-children-leaflet_NCB.pdf

[22] https://www.researchgate.net/publication/312600262_Creative_Thinking_among_Preschool_Children

[23] https://www.gutenberg.org/files/15114/15114-pdf.pdf

[24] https://discovery.ucl.ac.uk/id/eprint/1522668/1/Thesis%20Moulton%20V%20281016.pdf

[25] https://www.bda.uk.com/foodfacts/healthyeatingchildren.pdf

[26] http://www.tuskmont.org/uploads/1/7/7/2/17728377/follow_the_child_trust_the_child.pdf

[27] https://www.apa.org/pi/families/resources/develop.pdf

[28] https://extension.colostate.edu/docs/pubs/consumer/10249.pdf

[29] https://www.empoweringparents.com/article/risky-teen-behavior-can-you-trust-your-child-again/

[30] http://www.wecf.eu/download/2018/05%20May/WSSPPublicationENPartC-MHMchapter.pdf

www.ingramcontent.com/pod-product-compliance
Lightning Source LLC
Chambersburg PA
CBHW021142080526
44588CB00008B/171